Also by George Kalamaras

POETRY BOOKS
Marsupial Mouth Movements (2021)
Through the Silk-Heavy Rains (2021)
We Slept the Animal: Letters from the American West (2021)
Luminous in the Owl's Rib (2019)
That Moment of Wept (2018)
The Hermit's Way of Being Human (2015)
Kingdom of Throat-Stuck Luck (2011)
The Recumbent Galaxy (2010)
(with Alvaro Cardona-Hine)
Gold Carp Jack Fruit Mirrors (2008)
Even the Java Sparrows Call Your Hair (2004)
Borders My Bent Toward (2003)
The Theory and Function of Mangoes (2000)

POETRY CHAPBOOKS
The Shoes of the Fisherman's Wife Are Some Jive-Ass Slippers (2021)
The Mining Camps of the Mouth (2012)
Symposium on the Body's Left Side (2011)
Your Own Ox-Head Mask as Proof (2010)
The Scathering Sound (2009)
Something Beautiful Is Always Wearing the Trees (2009)
(with paintings by Alvaro Cardona-Hine)
Beneath the Breath (1988)
Heart Without End (1986)

CRITICAL STUDY
*Reclaiming the Tacit Dimension: Symbolic Form
in the Rhetoric of Silence* (1994)

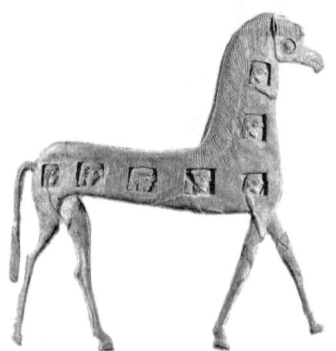

TO SLEEP IN THE HORSE'S BELLY:
MY GREEK POETS AND THE AEGEAN INSIDE ME

GEORGE KALAMARAS

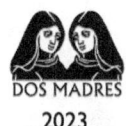

DOS MADRES

2023

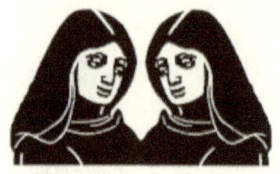

DOS MADRES PRESS, INC.

P.O. Box 294, Loveland, Ohio 45140
www.dosmadres.com   editor@dosmadres.com

Dos Madres is dedicated to the belief that the small press is essential
to the vitality of contemporary literature as a carrier of the new voice,
as well as the older, sometimes forgotten voices of the past. And in an
ever more virtual world, to the creation of fine books pleasing to the
eye and hand.

Dos Madres is named in honor of Vera Murphy and Libbie Hughes,
the "Dos Madres" whose contributions have made this press possible.

Dos Madres Press, Inc. is an Ohio Not For Profit Corporation and a
501 (c) (3) qualified public charity. Contributions are tax deductible.

Executive Editor: Robert J. Murphy

Illustration & Book Design: Elizabeth H. Murphy
www.illusionstudios.net

Front cover: the oldest known depiction of the Trojan Horse, seen on
the "Mykonos Vase" (*circa* 670 B.C.E.)
Back cover & p.147: "St. George on Horseback, Slaying the Dragon"
(*circa* 1425–1450 C.E.), iconography by Chanter Angelos Akotandos
(1400–1457 C.E.)
Author photo: Jim Whitcraft

Typeset in Adobe Garamond Pro & Trajan Pro
ISBN 978-1-953252-68-5
Library of Congress Control Number: 2022946915

First Edition

To Sleep in the Horse's Belly:

My Greek Poets and the Aegean Inside Me

TABLE OF CONTENTS

THREE
The Way Wolves Eat History When History Eats Its Young

FOUR
For My Family

FIVE
The Grammar of the Body

SIX

For My Family

SEVEN

Tiny Movements of the Throbbing World
Waiting for Us

EIGHT
For My Family

NINE
What We Speak Speaks Us

TEN
For My Family

ELEVEN
A Crush of Bees in Which to Bury the Tongue

Homage to St. Dionysios

for my grandparents,

George & Helen Avgerinos

and

Pericles & Stavroula Kalamaras

Wherever I travel Greece wounds me.
—George Seferis

here now I stand before all the Greek poets
—George Vafopoulos

I begin my song with the Helikonian Muses;
they have made Helikon, the great god-haunted
mountain, their domain . . .
—Hesiod

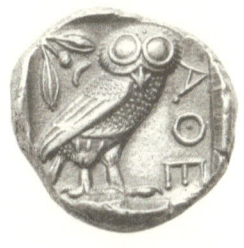

Looking for My Grandfather
with Odysseus Elytis

Looking for My Grandfather with Odysseus Elytis

I'm walking through the narrow lanes of Athens,
and Elytis is at my side, his right arm looped
through my left. His bald head, involved in some secret

triangulated message-sending with the full moon
and sunken sun. We are searching for Nono, the grandfather
I grew up with, George Avgerinos, though he has been dead

forty-five years. *Not here, not here*, Elytis says, gently
patting my hand, when I lean into a corner, when I crane
my neck into the *retsina* scent of a *taverna*, salivate

on the street near a woman in black and the turning spit
for a lamb, remembering my Nono, my brother Perry,
and me dividing the tongue into three even parts.

And though I don't believe him, I know he must be right.
Then we're in Zakynthos, the island of my grandfather's birth.
"The Poet's Island" Dionysios Solomos made famous

in 1822 and that now forever holds his name. Somehow
we've left Athens and have crossed the Ionian. Moonlight
resembles an asphalt bridge, lava floes of solidified sulfur

at Minerva Terrace in Yellowstone. I look back and watch
them dissolve in lapping caps and leaping hagfish. A Greek
Orthodox priest emerges from a glass coffin. He has seaweed

on his slippers. He wears a tiny gold cap; I sense that he is
old. He's St. Dan, greeting us in Demotic, saying something
about *hair shirts* and *stones in the mouth at Mount Athos* and *retsina*

wind carving cliffs and *lamb's tongue tucked safely in the chest
of every newborn foal*. His censer floats through Elytis,
and Elytis's cigarette suddenly catches moon-flint

and lights. *Not here*, he coughs, that hearty, tuberculous
cough of the many-smoked, thick clouds soaking us
both, the lava floes reemerging then disappearing within

the rasping strokes of the hagfish. We thank St. Dan,
kneel and kiss his feet. I hear something about *my son*
and *good boy* and *Mind that tongue in your own chest now too.*

Somehow both he and Elytis know my secret. That solstice
night in Colorado thirty-nine years ago when I kissed
the back cover photo of Elytis from *Maria Nephele*

before writing poetry, before logging the first vowel.
And then before sleep, kissing it again, slipping it
beneath my pillow, holding my right index finger

over the outline of his mouth as I curled into the darkness.
Drops of light, drops of light, I had silently chanted, echoing
Elytis's core, into moon-folds of sleep, into the sunken

yet persistent sun. And now both St. Dan and Elytis
look at me, each clasping two hands together in air
as makeshift pillows and, standing, rest their heads

upon them, saying in chorus, *Drops of light, Giorgos. Vowel without end, Giorgos. Tongue in the chest.* St. Dan returns to his coffin, caressing the hasp, seaweed stains

on the stones. Elytis takes me deeper into the island to a small village, a two-room hut. My great-grandmother Angeline on the floor, the midwife spreading olive oil

between her legs. Pans of boiled water. The lantern carving notches on the wall. *Here, Odysseus?* I ask, self-conscious that I've called him by his first name.

First the kiss, now thirty-nine years later assuming the liberty of his Christian name? He pats my hand, saying only my name in Greek, *Giorgos.* I remember the gamey taste

of tongue, eating it with my grandfather, asking why it was *I* who got his name. My great-grandmother moans, moon-flint again catching Elytis's cigarette. Something

like a lava floe stains the birthing rug. It is beautiful and terrible. My great-grandmother's face tightened as in orgasm or broken bones. I want to cry out, save her,

but I have no voice. Each time I go to speak, the ash on Elytis's cigarette glows more brightly, and something in my chest elongates through waves of saliva, crushing

my heart, caressing my esophagus, flaring the slate-gray lobes of my lungs. The midwife is now a giant fish, black shawl clasping the damp. Fierce gills pumping night wind,

forcing some rasp in the shape of, *Push, push!* Elytis holds
my hand, measures his breath to mine. He gently undoes
my trousers, the buttons of my shirt, dabs sweat

from my brow, rubs olive oil in slow circles on my chest
just above the heart where the crushing begins. *Push,
push*, he says. *Vowel without end in the chest*, he says.

Soon you will speak, Giorgos. Soon you will speak.

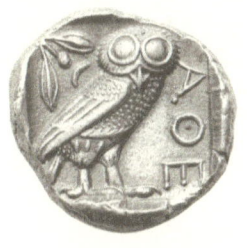

ONE

An Almost-Ovular Wailing

Nikos Engonopoulos Listens to Jacques Prévert's "Autumn Leaves" and Weeps

Quicksand slid into the back of his throat
There was an ocean in that mud, he knew,
But also piles of dead hummingbirds
He didn't know how to speak them
Back into life
He contemplated their wings
Begging some pause in the song to sink them
From his throat down into the sea caves
Of his chest
Where he might repair the feathers and heal
Their flight
Everywhere he turned it was autumn
The spring lilacs
Summer lightning
Christmas snow blistering the plane trees
Then came his mother's cancer
The way he rubbed her feet that week to ease her unrest
And his own
Then came his older brother, Athanasios
Dead from diphtheria
His father's gauzy eye
The time in bed with his first wife in the moon's half-light
When she told him she was pleased, but he did not believe her
He remembered Jacques Prévert
And their days in Paris
Cigarettes together at the café
Joking with Desnos, now dead
With René Daumal, gone

And René Crevel, also gone, though by his own hand
And Antonin Artaud's bit lower lip
Tristan Tzara's monocle
And days painting together with Giorgio de Chirico
Piles of dead piles of birds
Which he knew to be hummingbirds
Because of what he missed in the middle of the song
The throbbing wings the song evoked
In ways in which they were melancholic but gone
Gone the days of Athens cafés and art exhibits
Gone the dreams of writing of painting his dreams
Into a world he believed
Could be changed
When words in a sentence merged
When vexed verbs and the right noun
Cunning curves and color
But there persisted Prévert's "Autumn Leaves"
On the phonograph
Round and round like the seasons
Those leaves
As if they were barely holding barely clinging
To their russet their gold
Trembling
Falling
Sinking
With the birds
The piles
Of dead piles piling
Into the ground that he knew
Both bore him and would someday soon consume

Nanos Valaoritis Considers Trouble in the Tree of Life

We built this house ourselves, but others will inhabit it.
—Nanos Valaoritis

We built this tree ourselves, but others will eat it.
We built this brick, but others will place it in the cat's bed.
We built this bed, but others will deliver the daily mail from it.
We built the sky, the stars, even the ladder into the chasm,
but others will fly as they sink back through the gods.
We built our wars, which others will bless.
We built our building of peace, but others will weep.
We built a solution, but it will only dissolve.
We built our farms, but others will trouble the corn.
We built the corn certain that others might rescue the meat.

We built the *yes*; we built the *no*.
We built these words; we built this poem together.
Yet no one, no one will sit and break bread with it.
No one will come, confident and calm, to eat it.

Lemon Seeds of Yannis Ritsos

So you've heard that Yannis Ritsos used to sleep with tiny lemon wedges between his toes? That he'd roam the evening streets of Athens for the proper color—not quite wild-thrush yellow, not really marble green, never *Metaxa* brown? That he'd barter a leaflet of lamp-lit written socialist poems to have his paring knife sharpened just so, but always of delicate pulse on the blacksmith's stone? A sparrow might appear from flint chips, lift an instant and become the moon? Hay in the corner curving into the proud, pleading shape of a sickle? The blacksmith would begin feeding the leaflet, page by yellowed page, to the one old mare curiously nuzzling Yannis's lemon-scented pockets?

*

So you say you've seen Ritsos through the tiny apartment window return and pull, first, each acidic seed from his pockets, then the lemons, one by one, still whole yet somehow seedless? That the paring knife remained in a pen case on his desk beneath the lantern? That sparrows suddenly appeared outside in the geranium window pots like drops of anvil moon, flew through the jagged lightning crack across the pane, and became moths? That the linseed oil of the lantern flashed with the beating of wings and green velvet? And there was light?

*

You don't believe any of it, you say? Have never believed your own people could bleed? That Yannis Ritsos's tuberculosis could have been barbed into him by wire seeds? The kicks in the head and gut by officially approved junta fruit? Scars on his hands by jutted glasses of juice in which, imprisoned on Makronisos, he buried his poems to secure them from the guards? Yet now you also don't believe that you *don't* believe? It was the seeds, you say? The invisible fence within the pale plasma of a deranged geranium, choking out the light, even if it was only moon-glow? Your struggle to see them, abandoned, through strangling red leaves? The way the seeds seemed to seep pools of polished glass onto the mahogany table when he took up a pen and began to cut the rind and juicy pulp? First one lemon, then the next? Slice after slice? Then the door crack and pale glow and the tender bending after his bath, towel-slip to his knee, like a woman painting her toes? Wedge by saffron wedge? Eight seedless sickle moons? Eight moist edges, like the down of damp cotton balls between toes, that no longer touched? And afterwards, Yannis pausing on the stool, cigarette between two fingers, skin-shriveled from steam? Deep drags of afterbath smoke sinking and caressing his toes?

*

So you say you've heard and seen? That you believe and don't believe? That, inexplicably, the oil lamp on the table still smokes velvet green? That, though he's dead now, you're certain—or nearly certain—of the table stains, the ring of salt, the almost-ovular wailing, the seeds?

Michalis Ganas Looks at the Moon Looking at Him

Days come when I forget what I'm called.
—Michalis Ganas

So much civil war his head hurt
His father's head hurt
And his mother's
Even as a four-year-old his home in Epirus
In the border mountains of Greece seemed remote
Hawks circled their stone house, eagles, then vultures
Then bloody boar-like shapes drenched his dreams
In the Greek Communist retreat, they carried off entire villages
First they took him to Albania, then Hungary
The village of Beloiannisz
His mother wrapped deer offal in a pouch around his neck
His father prayed to St. George for family protection
Lanterns inside him turned moonward for a match
Little wood in the stove in Hungary to soothe their night
He helped strip wood from boarded buildings to burn for heat
As if cast into the middle of *Doctor Zhivago*
No wonder his poems are nostalgic even though he's lived
In Athens fifty years that he could measure in burned books
And when his wife shaves her legs now he hears screaming
From the gulags still and the fierce scraping of wind
And when his dog nuzzles his leg
He feels well-depths rise up to swallow him
And when starlight enters the window and bathes his knees
He sees death-drops disguised as rain against the pane
And when a friend phones
He worries about eavesdroppers and informants

So much war all he can do is call out to the moon
To write his poems for him
Yesterday he looked
He looked at it and begged it not to bleed
He rolled up his sleeve as if preparing
For a shot of morphine

Kazantzakis Finds in the Mirror the Face
of Zorba the Greek

First there was wind in his throat.

    Then he felt snowmelt from Mount Athos.

Donkey bray and rain-smoked cigars came from the *taverna*.

    The almost-voice of love in the streetwalker's stance.

There is a mirror in my throat, said Nikos Kazantzakis.

    And all the places without names.

He said you said I said.

    What if you looked in the mirror and saw an armadillo?

Monks from Mount Athos are said to have burned his books.

    And the dusty rains of the sirocco seared his brain

When they tore the pages

    Of *The Last Temptation of Christ*.

Sometimes Kazantzakis covered the mirror with a black cloth.

    Flowers. Frankincense. And morning processions.

Then there were bedtime openings as roads in his chest.

And he wept his head which wept the dark of his heart.

Once, Nikos swore he saw his reflection as sores in the moon.

Zorba dancing and singing and playing on the beach.

Mirrors, Kazantzakis insisted, *are two or more ways of mouth.*

What is agony? he kept asking.

What is the agony inside the agony of the wind—whingeing and hinged?

Miltos Sahtouris, Face to the Wall

Was it a directive   or simply description? A comma
commanded or   détente? Miltos Sahtouris
sat in his kitchen   carefully eyeing
his mirrored   hand. An electrical   hesitation
invaded him, as if a broken   rug   unbraided itself
in his spleen. *Cavafy*, he mumbled,   to no one
in particular. *Constantine lightning   from Alexandria,
constant—even now—in Athens*, he thought,   then became
delirious with the sound   of a death   spilled
        backwards.

                    Was it his own dissolve or a directive's?
Détente or   description?   The crazed Nile
or curved Aegean coral?   Seventy meters   deep.
                          Cotton braids or wool?
A carp caught on the rough edge   of the color
pink?   Miltos Sahtouris somehow   aspirated
only the absent *h* in   *Hydra*, then the   invisible
extra *th* of *Thessaloniki*.   Couldn't quite pry enough
hard consonants from *Nafplion*,   where the coming
of the Colonels   confused his lip. *All those sines
and only the chord   of the arc   of this tiny Athenian
apartment*, he heard,   from no one   no
one   in particular.

Descartes, he thought. The dermatome   of Descartes
in the   corner   grafted cliché after   cliché
upon   the sinew of a door.   *Surrealism,*
        Miltos confided,   *freed me from many things.*

16

Like the single spinal nerve   imitating slices
of skin. Like the command   that was his
       most moist vowel. The tendon that was   more
sound than substance   held.   Valve
that became the book it   spilled. Severed rooms
in the   severed memory   that no longer mirrored
his not-yet   severed hand,   no longer
instigated a hold,   digital and dispersed
of an acute angle   that equaled   the ratio
of the muscular power   of a hypotenuse. To no one
in particular. He thought   this, to no one
in   particular. Like any sensible man   of Athens
during the eerie calm   of the Colonels. Forced marsh
against the tepid of the tongue's   knotted spleen.

Comma obscene, or   command gleaned? Cotton
from Cavafy's Nile   or Aegean détente? Miltos Sahtouris
somehow aspirated the missing   *h* from the word *wall,*
the *h* buried in the snapped bone   of *face.* Wondered
if that absence was   a directive or description. Coral
or carp. Considered the marched spill   of his birth
in Hydra a long life   away, the cord
caught   on the rough edge   of the color
pink,   a primordial   tongue. As he sat
in an Athens apartment   far from the Colonels,
with no one in particular.   Staring   for air.

"The Circle of Hours":
Melissanthi's Hymnal Disposition

Only that among us the way up is the way down.
In order to ascend, we descend.
In order to approach, we retreat.
　　　　—Melissanthi

There are circles here. Circles
there. Summer becomes autumn,
and autumn becomes noon or
7:35 p.m. at the train station
or olives soaked in rainwater and brine.
There are circles within circles. Not
the clichéd kind, but a kind word,
say, trapped years in a vault.
When it is opened, pried, the word, too,
opens. And the person the word
passes into sometimes closes, if they had not
left the door to the basement ajar.
Bachelard saw circles. His attic,
a basement. His chest of drawers,
a piece of music. And Melissanthi
saw them by virtue of being
a woman. A woman who took a pen
name and no longer was
Hebe Skandalakis. No longer a woman
born in Thessaloniki, bastion
of Greek Orthodoxy.

There are many ways
to circle a circle. Many ways
to be human. Living in exhaustible sin,
for one, Melissanthi thought. Or waking
each morning, of course, with rain
in your gut. The mirror that pulls back
part of your face as if you continuously
stepped into wind. And the hours, too,
come back. Twice a day, as we all
know. Like taking twelve paces,
then stepping around swiftly
into a duel. We say we *kill time*. Maybe time
kills *us*, especially when we try to annihilate it
in our mouths with words we'd do better
to chew and swallow back into silence.

Melissanthi knew all this, raised
in the Orthodox faith. Studying
the Desert Fathers in Egypt who spent years
contemplating a stone, deciding
which side of the mouth to lodge it
in. *Behind the dam of silence, however,*
the same jumble of voices, she told us.
Should you board the 7:35 train
for Salonika, or the 8:32 to Heraklion?
O Melissanthi! O Hebe Skandalakis!
You were of two minds, two names,
two ways of carving
a notch in your once-stung heart
when it came to measuring
the rectangular weight
of a circle. Summer becomes autumn

each autumn. Autumn raising an army
of fallen leaves that in a rain-soaked wind
rise up to fight the night you knew
would soon descend. Drop
around and upon you
to devour your mouth.

O Pavlina!

The fibers of my voice stretch out
—Pavlina Pampoudi

Yes, your voice stretches out
Into me into
The trees
Where the wood thrush extends its chest
And becomes a grosbeak
You once said, *I have nothing to say to no one*
And my mind bends
Its attempt to suss out
The seeming double negative
Knowing there are no silences where you once
Spoke and keep
Speaking the trembling leaves
Because your breathing mists
The trees
Because your words remain alive in other people's bodies
Because if we do the math it all adds up
To a broken word
Spoken exact
Times two spoonfuls of table salt
That lathe the tongue
With moonlight and its miraculous mines
O Pavlina!
You eclipse the already-said
You step out into the dark
Of thinking you have nothing to say to no one
But having *everything* to say to the sound of now
And no one is there
No one is there to hear you

Zoë Karelli Freeing the Bones of the Dead

Mysterious and dreadful meanings, whispers from thence
—Zoë Karelli

Matutinal fire. Morning glory
burdening a vine with blue
from the inky depths
of the Aegean. The dead
are there. And the sad gold
fins. And the wavering
weeds. The dead, you told us,
never die.

Zoë. There are gesturing hands
and foodstuffs and trains
without whistles. Mouths
sewn shut. What did you hear
three years after your mother's death
when—according to Orthodox custom—
you disinterred her bones,
transferring them to the family
vault? What words passed between you
and your brother, poet Nikos Ghavril Pendzikis,
when you held her skull and drank deeply
thereof?

I imagine the world
the way the world imagines us.
I imagine the dead seeking shelter
in re-*membering* what it means
to be alive. I imagine your heart giving birth,
unfolding the fire of the first flower.

The Bedside Table of Angelos Sikelianos

Now we turn to the drinker of Lysol,
to the wrong bottle, to the   guilt-ridden
bedside nurse. Angelos Sikelianos refused
every platitude in favor of a luminous sea.
Sure, somewhere from the ether,   he still reads
about himself in the evening news;   every Athens
report on food inscriptions still somehow recalls him.

Here, check the ingredients of his   long-dead
mouth.   See if what he offered the world
might finally make us   see. Might urge the strong
coffee. Boil water for tea. Stimulate the unfolding agony
of the leaves.   If you ask him for a handkerchief,
he may be unsure he can produce the proper embroidery.
But if you request an apple every other Thursday at eight,
he can assure you of   the stethoscope's strain.

Okay, let's settle things once and for   maybe.
Tell the critics how Angelos   and his nurse
remain in that sickroom   as a gift
to the sea.   None of the clocks
near his bed admit their sand-hour   sad
to the opening   evening below. They keep turning
their hands through the luminous dark   of his poems
entangled in cypress leaves   in his bed,   his sheets.
Revealing wind-depths we know he   knew. There,
beneath Bachelard's floorboards.   The sleep sessions
of Robert Desnos—all the many   book bends
to Paris—   borrowing the mud   of Greek Tragedy
to stand on,   to redeem   what Angelos
and his sad, sad nurse   most joyfully need.

This Is Not George Seferis

. . . so much suffering, so much life,
went into the abyss
all for an empty tunic, all for a Helen.
　　　　—George Seferis

It was Athens. And it was hot. July 17, 1948. George
Seferis awoke inside his pipe. Felt the dawn-red glow over his
coals as sunset blue burning the back of his eyes. Was as large
and small as he could ever recall. Convex and concave cone
light. Carnival mirrors. He began fearing faucets, and the cat's
inquisitive sniff, and the dog's saliva, and the flat-backed ash-
stamping nail. Began craving *baklava* with burnt phyllo dough
and lamb stew, with the lamb smoked slowly over the pit.

George Seferis, yes, awoke that July day as a rod in the
retina of his left eye. Something long and pleading extended
from his mouth, *was* his mouth, and the entire vowel he tried
to extract from his bowl of *avgolemono* soup. *This is not a*
bowl of soup, he slurped, smacking loudly to diffuse the heat.
French writing sat on a plaque below the steaming bowl.
Syllabic smoke from the cursive. He wondered how he could
speak and not speak a simple Athenian vowel. How he could
and could not be Greek. How he might suddenly awake
and actually be his pipe, a rod in his eye. He investigated his
round white magnesium belly. He still loved Wallace Stevens
and probed by trying to sing beyond the genius of the soup,
but he kept hearing a blackbird in the sea-foam snows of
Olympus. He considered *Metaxa* and *ouzo*, but knew by now
that—though it was morning—it would always be last call

at the corner *taverna*, and that someone, anesthetized over
a game of chess, would be talking vulgarly while listening
to thunder come as Vedic chants. He remembered Eliot.
He remembered Pound. He remembered his wife and even
turned to the idea of sewing as a way to fix things and finally
make them right. But images of umbrellas on dissecting
tables kept cutting his attention to some castle and god-awful
contraptions of mold and metal clasps. Even Lautréamont
wrestling with a shark.

Yes, it was July. It was hot. The number 17 glowed like
someone's sunset in sea coral, in the coals. Even the soup was
beginning to drift toward something more solid. First, lamb
stew, and then toward things sweeter, his favorite custard,
galaktoboureko. Seferis struggled with being Greek. With being
born in Asia Minor. With being an exile from his *own* exiled
self. How to say it new without stirring that Florida Key in the
Fourth Quartet of Lautréamont's shoe. *Yes, to be a vowel,* he
thought. *To be a simple, complex mouth. To sleep in the horse's
belly just once during the prolonged night of an entire syllabic
pause with only a Helen!*

Cooking fires began to blaze below the wheels, then fade
beneath the hocks. There were spears stuck in mud, propped
against Trojan stone. Men and women were touching. A left
breast exposed. A tongue over someone's nose. An extended
vowel in the shape of a moan. And there was wine, and
spilling it, and sleeping it off.

Yes, George Seferis awoke inside his pipe. Inside his soup.
Peering out from the extinguished tunnel of his elongated
spoon. He still feared the faucet, the cat, the drop of drool,

the iron nail, the syllables of others already sunk like constant casks in his chest. He considered how he could speak and not speak the silkiness of potatoes in a lamb stew. How he could and could not be a simple Athenian vowel. Contemplated the belly, the wooden horse, the fires below, two unwound spools of sewing thread entwined like Hippocratic snakes at the base of an umbrella. The intermingling of bread and wine of the Sacred Liturgy. Even condoned the golden glow, the holy book, which the Greek Orthodox priest brought the following morning, lifted over him three times in the sign of the cross, kissed, opened, and read from to Seferis in Classical Greek:

> **meer-schaum** (mir-shəm, - ,shòm) n. **1.** A tough, compact, usually white mineral of hydrous magnesium silicate, H4Mg2Si3O10, found in the Mediterranean area and used in fashioning tobacco pipes and as a building stone. Also called "sepiolite." **2.** A tobacco pipe with a bowl of meerschaum. [German *Meerschaum*, sepiolite, originally the name of a kind of coral (Alcyonium digitatum), literally "sea-foam," translation of Latin *spuma maris* and Greek *halos hakhne*, "foam of the sea" (the coral was thought to be formed from congealed foam): *Meer*, sea, from Old High German *meri, mari* (see **mori-** in Appendix*) + *Schaum*, foam, from Old High German *scum* (see **skeu-** in Appendix*).]

    He kissed his hand. George Seferis kissed the priest's hand, thanking him for the prayer. He even stroked his index finger and thumb, calling him *Papa* so softly it almost hurt. To say. To hear. *So much sea-foam*, he thought. *So much coral. Seventy to two hundred fifty meters deep. Far too many wars. The deepening depth of despair. All for a Greek vowel. All for a Helen.*

Odysseus's Dog, Argos, Remembers
   What It Was Like to Be the Only One
   to Recognize Him Upon His Return

Because a hound dog, old, in a pile of cow manure,
with fleas. Because a hound dog, dead
for more than 2,000 years, remains alive
in dust-particles of thought. In the drumbeat
below deck, prodding the oars. In the rowing chemistry
of love in the ninety-ninth leg of a centipede.
Because we push ourselves
here, then there, one back-break at a time
until we arrive, achingly, at the place where oceans meet.
Because I came to him when no one else would.
Because *my* animal body recognized *his* animal body.
Because in smelling him, I smelled myself.
And I knew that what had been lost could always return,
even if it was gone, yet found in that leaving.
Because in the vortex where water collides we recall
the taste of our own urine—how drinking it yet again
cleanses it one more time before it is finally released.
Because the plants need to drink. Because the air
needs to drink. Because the water lily—
yes—also requires something upon which to float.
Aegean-strong of song. My hound-dog body—
though seemingly dead—buoyed, now,
all the way from Ithaca in the rise and fall
of the ribcage of the dog asleep on your own sofa.
In the shadow darkening the dark.
The shady places from which the Shades
speak with words bit

from light. The tender places you call home.
Because *everyone* needs a dog. And a past.
And the odyssey of moving here to there.
Back, always, to here
and a dead voice, alive, from across the river.
To feel the living
depth of the dead. Because he knew me,
and I knew him. Even in disguise.
My Odysseus cloaked as a beggar.
The grape pulp scent of his feet. The odor
of burning he carried all the way from Troy.
And the scent of that knowing was enough.
Is *always* enough. Even amidst the fleas
biting my body. And the bewitching voices,
in air, of leaves. And our animal bodies
strapped against the call.
Dog body. Man body. The body in between.
And all those beard years at sea.

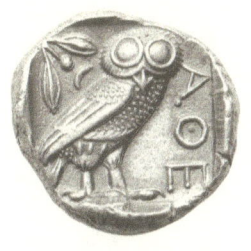

TWO

For My Family

Photo of My Great-Grandmother and Three Children
   Weeks Before They Board the Boat
   for the New World, *Circa* 1916

Yet another day when I ponder the dust, finger the rain.

This time, it's mud blotches on Nono's knickers.
Those two dark stains remind me
of what I carry of him—my grandfather—inside me.

Great-grandmother Angeline is clutching
Nono's sleeve. Trying to tame the animal
that has taken over the boy, the animal

that brought the entire village of Bohalis down
to the Zakynthos docks a few weeks later, cheering
that the boy and his wild ways were leaving.

His younger brother, Dan, looks confused.
Head cocked, ears he has not yet grown
into, eyes drifting in and out

of some foggy forecast
he's trying to hear in the shivering
leaves of the olives

about a New World, better food,
perhaps, and more to eat. Aunt Martha—
just a toddler in frilly dress—is holding

a tiny purse, as if the coming journey across
the Atlantic could be contained
in a little bag and one day make her

the kind of woman she adores
in her mother's cooked dandelion greens
with olive oil, lemon, and oregano. The cross

that hangs on great-grandmother's neck is large.
Looks heavy as the black peasant blouse
and long skirt that keep her

modest in a rural village where rumors—
not just the evil eye—can kill.
It rests across her breast like the weight

of Byzantium that somehow bolsters
yet breaks the daily bread
of the poor. Where is Stelios,

my great-grandfather, in this photo?
I imagine he's either at work in the factory
in Chicago Heights, or relaxing afterwards,

sipping *retsina* and smoking a cigar
in a tiny apartment, having already crossed
the ocean. Alone. He's waiting

just a few more weeks for the family
he sent for. He knows there is no going back
to little food and to what in America

might be called a shack. A war-ravaged
village, where Nono—my grandfather Giorgos—
used to sneak loaves of bread

past the Turkish troops, tying them up, tucked,
under the bellies of his goats. This is the dawn
of a dark world coming into view

with all the light of the Ionian Sea
tempering the photo, entering
my cells with dark, luminous light.

A sirocco blowing in from North Africa,
dusting the wind-whipped pines
with bits of sand all the way from Algiers.

Yet another day fingering the dark and its drenching
rain. My family is standing there, waiting for me.

Leaving Greece Before I Was Born and Coming
to the New World with My Grandparents
Pericles Kalamaras and Stavroula Demopoulos

1912 and 1921, respectively

As if the boats *Piraeus* and *Saturnalia* brought *me* here,
not just Pericles Kalamaras and Stavroula Demopoulos.
As if the veins of grape leaves tonight
on the wooden cutting board
were runnels of fallen ash
from Kepler-1649c. Earth's twin.
Where life may or may not
rill. As if coming to the New World
was like being yanked—potato-shocked—
from the ground and submerged in beet broth
for soup. As if *as if* was not just a comparison
but the way we learned to leave our words
back in Pharaklatha and Solaki, the villages'
war-stained strain, and entice the owl tongue
urging the boats across the ocean into a forest
of sound ground.

Papou. Yia-Yia. We had so little time
together. So few roasted lambs and bowls
of *avgolemono.* Yet the way you embraced
one another on a moonless night in Chicago
is still there inside the cells of my skin.
I did not have to cross the great water.
You did not have to cross the great water.
But you did, and I am here, writing you

about the ways you have written me. Written
into me the *saganaki* and *spanakopita*
of my name. *Kalamaras* comes from *calamari,*
squid. And to be a Kalamaras in Greece
meant to take up the squid's ink and write
something. *Anything.* With its sea-stained ache.

Yes, with the sea, we ache. We age. We ache
and age over and again. As if our seafaring
selves bring up the inky blue depths of all
that stirs. Beneath us. There, below the unsettling
waves. Where Poseidon pouts because we have come
that far. And in our coming that far his tempestuous
self knows we have also drawn close.

You have come. *We* have come. You
milked-loose one night a fierce act
of touching. And I am here, tendered from that
urge. Touching you. Again. As if the boats
Piraeus and *Saturnalia* brought the milky silt of my name up
from the sea-stunned froth. As if what is churned
from below—groin-fire, perhaps—
can somehow make a man through *others*—
when your son Vasilios kissed
my mother, Georgina. And they were born
unto me.

      I don't have a better way
to say it. To vowel and tender and ache, thanking
you—*Papou, Yia-Yia*—for loving the moon enough
to call its milk on a cloud-banked night
down into one another and through. The days

across the water must have been hard. The way
into the tongue of your grandson
must have been something you could barely have
conceived. The slog and donkey-sway
of your thick Greek vowels urging my liquid
English as you held me on your lap, feeding me
a spoonful of soup. Letting me taste a tongue
of roast lamb, the runnels and rills
of your flesh somehow there in the grape leaves
of *Yia-Yia's dolmades.*

                            Like the three hearts of a squid
pumping below your boats all those sea-knots
long. Its eight arms swirling through the murky
depths, pointing to Pharaklatha and Solaki
and Chicago and this moment of ink all at once.
Its eight arms reading the Braille
of the sea, pleading with the dark,
reaching toward you. Toward me.
Even toward the depths that have slowly named us
momentarily into these brittle bodies.
That will one day reclaim the tough and tender
of our tongues into a dissolve
the wake of bees, of what we believe
to be ink. There, below the rise and fall of the unsettling
waves that will surely one day settle us into the certain
uncertainty of the world.

They Brought the Stone

They brought the stone containing my birth date and the outline of a river's curves. I kissed it, clutched my navel, called it *Stavroula*, called it *OM*, referred to it as *best bird's beak in my chest*. I pictured my grandmother from Solaki when she was old and could barely remember my name, asking if it was *candle* or *crayon* or *less than or equal to*. The stone was cold, hobbled my lower lip with a hexagon of hired hieroglyphics, constrained roses and uncompleted hyphens, and the mournful scroll of *belovèd whooping cough* and *devoted devotee of fly-squat and cranes*.

Someone told me my icon had begun to weep sandalwood paste. St. George covered in the cremation ash of a Ganges River sadhu. Something was trying to live or die. Some tanager throng in my chest. Over and over. They beat its wings with a broom. They beat its wing, calling me *traitor*, *turncoat*, even saying I was speckled, brown, and blind. That my name had never been *Giorgos*, after all, but *starling* or *sparrow stew* or *soggy Indiana ground*, perhaps only the revolving wind whoosh of *ooh* and *aah*.

The stone was the exact weight and sphex of my lip, minus (of course) the stinging. I knew I could use it to startle the town into lightning, to chew jagged milk from a goat, to soak the hind leg of a fly into a hexagon of great good fortune. I cursed its scrawl and subsequent scratch, gripped its birth-date bliss with every Sanskrit grain that graveled my chest, with each blessing born from the rake and screw and almost-sound uttered from the thorax-fix, lodged at length—but released at last—from the smiles and fibrillations, from the catnap scratch of waking sleep and long years of the throat.

On the Origin of God: Tales from the Village of Solaki

So it was—in the time of dim light.
I remember 1961, asking during
the oceanic swirls of my bath,
Who created God, Yia-Yia? My grandmother,
stern with a five-year-old. *That's a sin
to even think about.*

                  And so it came to pass
that starlight entered the mouths of the dead.
That I was warned never to lay a hat
on a bed. Not to open an umbrella
in the house. To never give away a knife—
sell one for a penny if need be—or someone
might cut themselves. Never leave a pair
of scissors open to invite bad luck,
or give perfume as a gift without receiving
a coin. And when you say *Yeia mas*—cheers—
you may do so with wine, water, even milk,
but *never* do so with coffee.

                  Those days
of understanding my newly formed body
were awkward. Dim. Winding into me
like every snake I was told to fear. There was darkness
in every corner. Weather to ward off.
Animals lurking I had not yet known
to name. But I remember the clean scent
of Ivory soap. The bathtub on Chicago's
South Side. Even the rubber stopper

Yia-Yia would place in the drain, carefully,
like the great stone across Christ's tomb.
But if God created everything, Yia-Yia,
I persisted, *who created Him?* Again, I was warned
to mind my thoughts. To never even *think*
such things.

And I was taught to make sure
I never mistakenly gave the evil eye, careful
to say, *Ptou sou*, while giving a compliment—
short for *Ptou sou na min se matiaso*,
meaning, *I'll spit on you so I don't put
the evil eye on you.* To never cross
my legs at a funeral, or leave my shoes
lying on their sides. Careful to never
let salt, bread, or eggs leave the house after sunset.
And to always leave through the same door
of any house through which I had entered.

Yes, we enter many homes in the dim
light of our knowing. Our trying
to find out. From caves and lean-tos,
to rings of stone with animal hides
and still-smoldering fires. Our unknowing
walking arm in arm down the aisle
with what we think we know. Many rooms
into which we should spill salt into doorways.
There is much to be feared, I learned over
and again. Many stars to weep. Cloth *filaxta*
charms to be pinned to a dress. Placed in a pocket.
Garlic to be hung. Spitting to be done.
Pots of food never to be eaten

directly from. Pomegranates each New Year's Eve
to smash. The creation of God
to be a question dutifully ignored.
Many slices of bread that if dropped to the floor
must quickly be picked up and kissed.

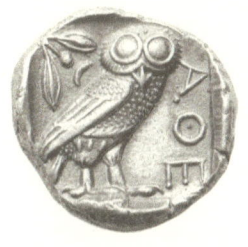

THREE

The Way Wolves Eat History
When History Eats Its Young

The Madness of Michael Mitsakis

A hummingbird entered your throat,
and you went mad. So much for 1896 and swollen

toes. For the flaking of skin you had been
convinced was your insides trying to cry.

If I was asked to kiss you, I would immediately
defrost bees from the freezer and lovingly send

them swarming to Algeria where you might have
crossed the sea to cultivate sanity. The forgotten

remain forgotten. Especially a journalist like you
whose associative poems crowded the owls

from their resinous midnight release. What word,
what fracture of color, did you see

those last twenty years when you were institutionalized
and babbled moon to moon? Some said it was just another

poem. The wind knew better, bringing
the clockflower into your mouth so you could

tell time by the seasons. You were a Surrealist
before the wing-beat of Java sparrows pulsed blood

into the mouths of André Breton.
Michael Mitsakis, lost to us.

The way wolves eat history when history eats its young.

Nikos Gatsos and a Certain Fatigue in the Color Green

Dark and great loneliness with so many pebbles round your neck,
so many coloured stones in your hair.
—Nikos Gatsos

Sad road, dust road, chauffeur-driven car. Weekly,
      he'd travel from Athens to Asea with a bouquet
of lilacs for his mother. Then Nikos Gatsos
      would drive straight back to Athens. Was it the scent
of her hair in a pale green scarf that drew him,
      that brought him out like the elongated entrails
of a bee? Some pebble round his or whomever's silk
      swan neck? A private lunging in his abdomen?
Or in that rumbling vowel that edged him
      each morning to Flocca's Café to sit inside
at a downstairs table, most remote from the door,
      removing sesame seeds one by one from his toast?
His toast, *dead* toast. His mother's moist swan dust flavoring
      the car's seat as east or west or as any grain of salt?

Nikos was like the sweetest of grandfather elephants
      or the wisest and most fastidious of tortoises, the goatherd
said, sipping an afternoon *ouzo* while sitting
      at an outdoor café in the old settlement, Asea,
where Nikos had been born. *But besides writing*
      Amorgos, *he died empty of poems, full—instead—*
with penning popular songs. Curved song, swan bone,
      rubbing against the goatherd's left knee as goat-bleat
or fur. *Imagine dedicating a book, "to a green star,"* he continued.
      But he died penniless, they say, gambling off even his library.

What *is* the sound of a green star dying?
        Of thousands of thunderbolts disintegrating
into the thick, ponderous folds around an elephant's
        leg? Of the backgammon board branded in zigzag
tortoise crack? Of the echo, *Kill me now!* sloshing—like wine
        in a ship's cask—in a die, rolled against a back alley
wall, as you beg for the luck of one dark eye? To be buried
        in the Asea of your birth in the same cemetery
as your mother is to refuse the dissolve
        of a sugar cube at an outdoor café? To lie
there in the grass forever next to your lame cousin
        who never left the remote province is to carry in
your pocket names of former lovers from Athens,
        to cut and paste them at random with words
from your stamp collection? Is to cast a sesame seed
        as a pebble from around the neck? Cry out
for vowels like a deaf man into a spark of kerosene,
        Give me the nuzzle-grove lamp of a stinging jellyfish?
Who, after all, really was Agathi Congo? Senegal
        Dimitrouka? U.S. Katsimbalis? Katerina
New Guinea? Papua Embirikos? And how might
        a poet who sank in Asea with mother and cousin,
who wrote only one great poem, collapse
        for forty-nine years into the interior
of the color green? How does the consistency
        of salt agonize the rolling thread of a pair of dice
into the single nerve at the base of the spine, further up—
        even—into nerve ganglia at the medulla oblongata?

Green star, *dead* star, bee in the left and right
        hair of this mother. Of that lump of lilac.
Of that riddle of a monkfish somehow buried

"face down" in thickening petroleum jelly.
Which side you see is always a matter of perspective,
          imbued the astrologer, turning the cup
over to reveal golden entrails of a bee swallowed
          by a swan that refused sesame seeds and flight.
To live and live until you're seventy-eight, knowing
          that you died at twenty-nine? *Who among us would*
not gamble not only his library but even his underpants?
          asked the stone camped in the mouth of a priest
at Mount Athos. *I'm not sure. I'm honestly not sure,*
          answered a sudden fatigue in the color green,
dispersed as warm, milky starlight throughout
          the fiercely plagued plains of the dead man's chest.

Matsi Hatzilazarou and the Taxidermies of Sleep

You woke mornings, convinced a peacock
had been sewn slantwise into your chest.

As soon as the shadow of darkness darkened,
saliva stirred the well-depths below your tongue.

And poems emerged. You looked at your husband.
He became a kerosene lamp tilted in the straw.

There are criminal forests, and there are
gamblers at the *taverna* who prefer to nap.

Someone told you that Brahms would bring you
fish and salt wrapped in the leaves of a strangler fig.

Now my throat tightens as if you brought me a photo
of my grandfather and his seventeen windows to the sea.

Let's look out for one another, Matsi. It still bothers me
that your husband, Andreas Embirikos, treated you

in psychoanalysis, then married you. Bachelard's fire
must surely be conversing with the wind, troubling

the black branches of the north. There are words we tell
no one. Each, cut and diced. Once, as a child, I told

my mother over and again that I needed to kiss the furry spot
of every moth that had killed itself against the glass.

Psychoanalytic Session in Which Andreas Embirikos Treats His Future Wife, Matsi Hatzilazarou

AE: Okay, shall we begin?
MH: What is time anyway?

AE: So you have said that you've not been sleeping?
MH: Once, when I was a child, I stepped on a snake in damp grass and knew I'd one day become a poet.

AE: Poetry, then, for you means what?
MH: Imagine a mathematician cleaning latrines, a shopkeeper in the physics lab, a street musician performing *rembetika* while giving the Church's last rites to the not-yet-born.

AE: I admire the metaphors. Can you say more?
MH: In other words, you have ten fingers and ten toes but want to count higher?

AE: You answered my question with a question. Are you aware of that?
MH: Yes. No. Perhaps?

AE: Let's discuss your father.
MH: My favorite vegetable is chocolate. My favorite soup, moon-bathed mud.

AE: You seem hesitant to discuss your father? Did you find his male voice oppressive? Is that what has guided you into the watery realms of Surrealism?
MH: There's nothing hesitant about starlight held in the mouths of the dead.

AE: I agree. Breton and Desnos would find your words startlingly beautiful. Once, when I lived in Paris, they told me that the most marvelous image is both alive *and* dead.
MH: Is that a question?

AE: Say more about your readings of the philosophies of the East. I hear tinges of Zen koans at times in your responses.
MH: What is the sound of one question answering itself, just in the asking?

AE: Again, you're answering with questions?
MH: Please, be kind?

AE: Okay, then, tell me how you first came to Surrealism.
MH: I think I'm falling in love with at least three of your two ways of mouth. I see four swans in your eyes, five of which are content not to fly away.

AE: Your relationship to the Church?
MH: George. My icon is that of St. George.

AE: Now we're getting somewhere. You mean the one where, on white horse, he slays the dragon?
MH: You seem stuck in your mouth. Stuck in your own mouth. To an ever-clanging bell. A church bell.

AE: Meaning?
MH: I don't think he *slays* any dragon.

AE: You're trying to say?
MH: Consider the dragon not evil. Not a representation of sin. Nor a fallen angel carved into the mouths of debt. Think

of the yogis of India. What if the dragon was the Kundalini energy they describe? Let's say George—*St.* George—holds a spear to represent his spine when sitting in quiet meditation. Say he thrusts it into "the mouth of the dragon" (what yogis would call the serpent power coiled at the base of the spine, waiting to unwind). Say he's not slaying anything evil but drawing Kundalini up from the lower chakras into the higher regions of knowing.

AE: Fascinating. I know you've studied the teachings of the East, but I never thought that a person might . . .
MH: Is a person a person or just droppings of horse-flies and swans?

AE: The swans you said were in my eyes?
MH: My favorite fruit is chocolate.

AE: Have you ever considered taking your "madness" to Paris?
MH: I want only to marry the wind in your mouth when you stop talking and say absolutely something.

AE: What, though, would be there but a proposed emptiness?
MH: Consider false teeth on the nightstand of the agèd. Rubbing alcohol, fungus, and a boiled egg. Who is speaking whom when we dream it is the dream dreaming *us*?

AE: I find you one of the most fascinating cases I've ever encountered in my practice.
MH: When we look at the Holy Icon, we focus on St. George. We tend to forget the horse upon which he rides. But is it George or the white horse underneath him coming to save the world?

AE: And that's important because? You know, we all ride

something or someone at some time or other.
MH: But what's there? Who, whom, or which? Seferis said, *all
for a Helen*. Trojan Horse, I ask you, or our wingèd bleed?

AE: I'm not sure I'm following?
MH: The horse's belly is full. And I grieve for the hungry
in the streets. But what is there? Inside. Inside the insides of
things. Ah, how beautiful—to sleep in the horse's belly.

AE: The beauty of your beautiful words is truly most beautiful.
MH: How lovely. How gorgeously sad. How beautifully sore
the lonely silences between and within your words.

Athos Dhimoulas and a Certain Strain of Rain

There are pieces of carpet still in his mouth from when
he got down on all fours and tried to sniff out the sanctity

of the world. Bookshelves beckoned him. Train whistles.
In which Joan Miró came, amoeba-like, begging for a glass

of water in which to submerge himself. So many things
perplexed Athos Dhimoulas. Pharmacies. False teeth.

Tobacco factories suggesting midnights alone on the fire
escape counting his life. Poems circulated from the Greek

underground, describing a man who was an egret in public
and secretly a pine tree when alone at night. Athos often

wondered whether he'd spent a former life as a monk
on *Holy* Mount Athos. Then rain, and patterns on his shirt

would elongate checks into shapes both giraffe and Bactrian.
Mirrors came and went. Possibilities became the hindquarters

of Moroccan tagine chicken he could tear apart and eat. *Death
of Death The*, was said backwards, in passive voice, in ways

which resembled bees swallowing themselves in their flight
from Mount Olympus. Dhimoulas sat eating *loukoumades*.

Each donut sprinkled not with honey and walnuts but with
words of his poems found missing at the depot. Carpet

fibers, rain-soaked with regret, left shredding in his mouth.

Katerina Angelaki-Rooke Contemplates the Words of Her Godfather, Nikos Kazantzakis

There is a fishbone caught in her throat
The size of a quarter moon
The triumph of constant loss, she said
Is a winter inside the coagulation of spring
Beautiful the moon and beautiful the dahlias
To be born in Athens among all those gods
To wake some mornings with red hair, others with brown
And breathe bus fumes crowding the Acropolis at noon
Blessèd be the fire ants of Namibia
Who forage for only seven minutes, thirty-three seconds a day
The scorching sand and heat is enough
To blister anyone who tries to write
A life
Who attempts the holy mountain
Trek inside
These are the things she thought
The things she became
Reading *The Odyssey* of her godfather, Nikos Kazantzakis
Spilling his words among crowds in Harvard, Iowa, New Delhi
The moon is some beached fish
She surely must have said during a lecture
Or some nights swallowing hard
Writing her poems of goldfinch blood and calm
Her poems of victory and deafening defeat
And long nights lantern-cast back through her own soothing
Yet disquieting dark
Translating Kazantzakis's *The Suffering God*
Like a god herself working
To understand herself and the swallowings of night
Near a flickering lamp casting its light darkly through her own

The Song of Love

based on a painting, The Song of Love,
by Giorgio de Chirico, 1914

Let's say there's a Greek sculpted head, a surgeon's
glove. A small green ball, threatening as an almost-tornado
sky. Let's say all three could crowbar the mind apart

like the fortuitous meeting of a sewing machine
and an umbrella inside a dead pigeon. No wonder
André Breton gave his wife, Simone, a photograph

of this painting to commemorate the night they merged
with the moon three times in just three hours,
thirty-three minutes. Two of the three objects

are mounted on a wall. Was he telling her
the third time made him round as the color green
absorbing stormy Earth's sound? In the distance,

a locomotive. Always, for de Chirico,
a locomotive. Somehow the smoke
of arriving was always a form

of departure. He came into this body
part Greek. When he left, the world
knew him only as Italian. The way

Breton entered the marital bed
a Surrealist and emerged a Java sparrow
inside the woman inside his satisfied man-body.

Let it rain, de Chirico once said,
when he meant to say the word *love*.
Touch me where it hurts, he blurted,

when he longed for love and its desperate
wing-beat release. He was a Surrealist
before the Surrealists. Like being Greek

prior to the plains-torn wars
at Marathon. At Thermopylae. Like a song
in which we float many months

before we emerge, screaming and weeping,
from the woman's dark. Like a classically
sculpted head before thoughts think us

into the terrible tissue of night.
This was Giorgio de Chirico.
Part howl. Part vowel. Part Greek

without the ruins of Rhodes to confiscate his calm.
Like *The Song of Love*, known to Breton
as *Le chant d'amour.* Seen in the endless smoke

of arrival and departure. Of a name. Of a dead pigeon.
Of being Greek. Of the cradle and its earthy urge. Stirred
inside the stirrings of the moon with Simone Kahn as the word

love. Before the painting's building and its dark
arches—to which we are always nailed—
fall in concussive collapse.

Yorgos V. Makris' "An Attempt to Become Enchanted"

*Makris found it impossible to exist save in the most authentic
immediacy.*
      —Nanos Valaoritis
We are the harbingers of chaos.
      —Yorgos V. Makris

1.

They say he was the Jacques Rigaut or Jacques Vaché
of Greek Surrealism. His mysterious poem, "An Attempt

to Become Enchanted," lost. Never to be discovered,
even read. By anyone. Still, years before Makris' suicide,

poets were convinced they'd encountered the urge
of his dirge. André Breton swore the poem

wrote itself *into* him one night in a dream. It began,
he recounted, *Think of all the umbrellas unfolding lotuses*

in the spine. Andreas Embirikos argued the impossibility, saying
Makris never liked lotuses, partial as he was to sunflowers.

Across the city, Robert Desnos confided the poem's closing
came to him one rainy night while passing an unknown

woman on the street. Trench coat belted tight
at her waist, her long hair extending in wind, whipping

across his face, he heard the words, *And so, it all comes to this?*
Benjamin Péret, whose translation of Paz's *Sunstone* Makris

56

used for his own translation of Paz into Greek,
announced during the period of hypnotic sleeps

that Makris' poem had silently entered his throat
when René Crevel recited Homer to those assembled,

though Péret could not speak Makris' poem,
only moil through its form. *Surely,* he noted,

it is a Surrealist sestina, so trangressive
it is written as a villanelle coaxed into heroic couplets.

2.
Sure, Simone Kahn sat combing her hair
one afternoon at the Bureau of Surrealist Research,

convinced Makris' "An Attempt to Become Enchanted"
was not lost but revealed itself at 15 Rue de Grenelle

the evening Suzanne Césaire sat across the room, crossing,
uncrossing her legs. The dark swish of her hose

emitting the sound of rain caught in the gutter
of a sparrow's throat. Makris remained silent about it all.

Even before his death. And Embirikos was again adamant.
Asserting that Yorgos Makris never liked rain or gutters

or the dimming copper of sunset impersonating a woman's
tights. Or even coal mines canaries festered when they flapped,

unwittingly, into the wing-beat dread of the dead. What *was*
this enchantment, the French wanted to know?

Éluard and Soupault straining to decode Makris'
words over a game of chess or while listening to one another

gulp a glass of soda water between the interludes of Bach.
And how might they conjure the healing waves

of Greek dissent lingering in the marble struggle inside
the classical parts of their own throats? *Stay alive*

awhile longer, Yorgos, members of the group would say,
though not in words but in their own enchantment

with Delvaux and the curves of blank-faced
classical women his paint brush coaxed and stroked.

Suicide was not an answer, they knew.
It had not brought Rigaut or Vaché closer

to the fertile forests of Transylvania and surely would do
Makris no good. Though they knew all too well

that René Daumal kept practicing death,
huffing carbon tetrachloride to retrieve the unknown.

3.
Put simply, the Surrealists were stumped,
even when convinced they kept hearing

Makris resurrected, even before his death,
in the vowel and split of what they had been told

had been lost. Gone. Nailed to the trees' wind. So much
for the dark forests of what they took for sleep.

So much for sleep itself, which they began to regard
with warranted suspicion. So much for Yorgos Makris—

the Greek incarnation of Rigaut or Vaché—even though
he and his forever-lost poem were never read but kept

appearing at odd moments, materializing smoke
in wind, laying its enchantment into their bodies

at the opera. At the docks. Into colors
of a Remedios Varo apparition. At the thought

of Georges Bataille frequenting back alleys
and Paris brothels. Even as they cleansed

at night in the tub, trying to decide which
was more enchanting—the warm bathwater

in which they soaked, or the words of a lost Makris
poem Embirikos swore could be their salvation

(if they could but finally hear it) coming to them in fragments.
As if their minds, themselves. Were fractured. Their mouths.

Only able to absorb parts of what the moon chose to bestow.
In its ongoing struggle between dark and more dark.

George Themelis Learns to Say, *I Love You*

And what sort of thing would God have been?
. . . What would Death have been without us?
—George Themelis

George Themelis took suck
from the crop milk at the base
of the neck of Alberti's burning
owl and from the charred part
of René Char's heart—both of whom
he had translated. Say a manta ray
beached itself on the island
of Samos as a way to claim
the flames. Say Nicolas Calas—
first named *Nikos Kalamaris*—decided
it was cannibalism to eat
the holy squid from which
he got his name. It could be
Japan and the slaughter
of dolphins that alerted
George Themelis to the importance
of taking footpaths with Orthodox
hermits in the Scetes Desert
of Egypt. They spoke Koine
Greek and Demotic Egyptian
as if the Tower of Babel
found, finally, the two true tongues
when it collapsed, crumbling to the ground.
Anthony the Great was a person
and a poem. And George Themelis

knew it was a form of writing when he prayed
to the saint that the desert might yield
cactus milk in his own heart too.
How to learn to say, *I love you*, in every language
of the world was Themelis's goal.
Though he never said so
but expressed it with the way
he hung his washrag, delicately,
after the bath. And wrote poems
as a translation of holding hands
with a moon split in two,
with a piece of burning straw
that sought and found its own drop
of water. *Outside of us*, he said, *things die.*
Animals die from anonymity
and birds from silence.
Which could be one reason
he married Alberti's owl.
And found in Char the burning
brain to seek God inward
as if he, too, were a monk
whose feet bore blisters
from the desert rough and sand.
Rilke wrote, *Only what's inside is near,*
the rest is far away. And Themelis
knew this in the sinking of his ink,
though he'd never read those words.
Instead, he wrote, *Whatever my soul*
has heard / Within me, it hears, as if
a letter directly to St. Anthony. As if
resuscitating dolphins with a basket of squid.
As if the inward deserts of Egypt

were storms confusing the sea, and he lived
in them both—all lightning long—walking
the waves and sand hand in hand
with what he knew had to be inside him.

Nikos Skalkottas Dies in Athens
   of a Ruptured Hernia, 1949

There was, of course, the sunken ship you woke one morning
to find Jason and the Argonauts in your chest. Modification

is often mixed. Confusion of seawater and notes. Which is why
you went to Berlin in 1921, to study atonal sound. How a note

could leave the expected, merge two or more ways of mouth.
Like Medea marrying Jason, then murdering their sons.

You were of two minds, Nikos. Romanticism yet fractured
notes. Like Cavafy's fish-bone poems stuck in Surrealist Greek

throats. That's why your breakdown brought you closer
to truth. Even when the public was confused

with your orchestral shifts. Now you are lauded,
though you died at forty-five with a parasite in your brain.

Even weather abandoned you to wind. Ceaseless, we blow
here to there, searching for the Golden Fleece. And many

times we kiss the wrong mouth in the search for our own
true song. Tongues are there. Probing. Intertwined. Like wind

and rain. Sun and less sun. Which history did you die in?
From which history were you eaten? Time is often confused,

if we believe Herodotus and his biographies of the violin dead.
When you died, you fell back in time into the Iranian Plateau,

seeking refuge in the dried blood of Medea's murdered sons.

Nikos Kavvadias, Seafaring Poet, Sails Around the World So Many Times He Becomes the Sound of the Sea

Down in far Port Pegasos
in this season rains are falling.
—Nikos Kavvadias

It was the sea   the sea   the sound

                                        of the sea

It was the sea   the wind

                  the rain   in the sea

It was the   sea the   swells

            emptying into   the sea-groan

                        ground   of the sea

He   was the sea

                  the brine   the wind inside

      rain   inside   seaweed scrapings

                        of the sea

Melpo Axioti and a Theory of Moths

You are the shadow of a goldfinch
trapped inside a slab of concrete.

The bones of your face groan
with the sudden burden of trees. Louis Aragon

and Pablo Neruda still call you *Sister*.
The Greek Civil War was a songbird

you soughed into a cage. Your exile gave the plane trees
an excuse to weep. Now the critics praise

your communism, your bread and water,
the color of your hair. Fumes from buses

perfume you. Footsteps fertilize the paper bags
on which you wrote your poems. All those years

of exile allowing the sound of your mouth
to retract. Even when it branched out

and became a library of drowsy moths.
Stop! Stop the train from tracking

words in your throat and taking them
through backcountry agonies

to East Berlin. Pablo Picasso puts down
his brush and paints you with his eyelashes.

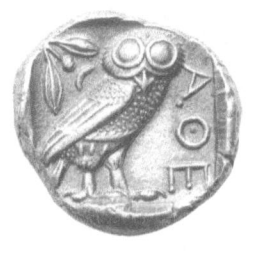

FOUR

For My Family

Nono's Shepherd Staff

for my grandfather George Avgerinos, 1904–1978

Spring again
Indiana lilacs are blooming
Worms coming alive
In the soil
In our bodies too
Shagbark hickories looking less like old men
In the fresh sun-bit light
My grandfather, Nono, wrapped in serape
Shepherd staff in his left hand
Planting a third foot
Walking me back through our grapevines
Something lush and entangled there
Telling me again about Odysseus
And the wooden horse
And how clever he was to sleep in the horse's belly

I want a horse too
Like Alexander's Bucephalus
Something large and dark
A blaze across the forehead
I want to grow up and be wise like Alexander
Who turned wild
Untamed Bucephalus toward the sun
And calmed him from his own stalking shadow
I want a horse as cunning as the men who hid
Inside the wooden one inside the gates of Troy
Undetected

And won the ten-year war
Going home to a wife like Penelope who wove
And unwove her tapestry each evening
As if she were untangling herself in moonlight
Until her man returned
Smelling of brine and burnt wood

*

Mary Ann laughs and says / though second-generation /
sometimes I still act like a first-generation / immigrant kid /
the boat across / seemingly just a few years / back / the
umbrella I refuse to open / in the house or the hats / I never
lay on a bed / or the way I won't tell a bad dream in the
morning / until I've had a bite of bread or a bit of tea / for fear
of the dream coming true / and the things I save like a
ripped coat / or frayed shoelaces / which I'm certain I may
one day need / to tie together to get me by / for a day perhaps
or two / in the event the new ones break / the ties of family
for me / themselves worn, frayed

*

How fortunate to have lost a father
To Sunday visitation, Greek Easter, Thanksgiving,
Father's Day, and two weeks in August
Before the start of school
To have fallen into this serape-wrapped man before me
Walking me back through the woods
His tales of Odysseus, Leonides and the three hundred
Spartans at Thermopylae
Lessons of Aesop
Plato's cave and what it means to step from the dark damp
Into a set of warm bones

But it's the shepherd staff I still see
Clear, all these decades late, as an Indiana moon
Snagged on an oak
Nono just beginning to slow
With his staff as a third leg and the Sphinx's riddle
In front of Thebes he loves to retell
What goes on four feet in the morning
Two feet at noon
And three feet in the evening?
A wooden staff from the Old Country
Given to him some years after he left
Recalling when he tended goats
Coming back to me now
The curved handle
Shapes painted in tribal village designs
Even after I lost it eleven years ago in the Colorado wildfire
Knock on wood
I had the wooden staff so long
Knock on wood
It kept me straight and made me brave
As Perseus facing Medusa
Strong as Hercules completing the twelve impossible labors
The shepherd staff
My own wooden horse
From which I could emerge
Victorious
Knock on wood
Was the signal the cunning men used
To alert one another it was time to open the horse's belly
And descend upon the drunken sleeping hordes

And there is Nono again taking my hand
Propping the staff against a branch
Measuring the vines

Tendering a few careful clippings
Reminding me what Aesop said
In "The Fox & the Grapes"
"The Shepherd Boy & the Wolf"
Lord knows I had a lot to learn
Lord knows I still do
Lord knows I needed a man from the island of Zakynthos
And the ways of the woods
Brought into me
The seasons
The turning smoke from the slash pile we burned
Twice a year
Down near the swamp
Where raccoons and water moccasins thrived
Where we ignited the night
Crackling flames
Mirroring the flash of lightning
Bugs
Drafts rising
From the flight of an owl
In an Indiana woods
A barred owl that could startle
When the throaty sounds began
That could be Athena, Nono told me
There to calm and help me see the dark
In the dark
And through it
Athena, messenger to Hercules
So that with or without leaning on the shepherd staff
All these years late
I might one day be able to face the Lion
Slay the Hydra
Capture the Cretan Bull

Bucephalus, Belovèd Horse of Alexander the Great

circa 355 B.C.E.–June 326 B.C.E.

To sleep. Soundly. Asleep.
    To sleep in the horse's belly.

No, not the Wooden Horse, Epeius and Odysseus's pride.
Left on the shores of Troy as ships seemed to sail home but
harbored instead at the nearby island of Tenedos. Horse of
cleverness and cunning in which hiding men waited to stun.

Not St. George's courageous white.
    The dragon of desire blazing from below.

Not even the wind. Storms tromping sails.
    White caps galloping the sea.

But Bucephalus. Ancient Bucephalus. Belovèd of Alexander.

Dear Bucephalus. Whether you are buried in Phalia or
Jalalpur Sharif remains unknown. It is all the same. You
continue to fill the soil of the Punjab.

Only thirteen-year-old Alexander could soothe you, turning
you toward the sun so you'd no longer fear your shadow.

To sleep. Soundly.
    To sleep in the belly of the wind. Belly of the dark.

To climb upon the magnificent
    and most memorable.

Yes, Philonicus the Thessalian offered you to King Philip for the sum of thirteen talents. Not even a Macedonian king could tame you. It took a thirteen-year-old boy.

My grandfather first told me. At the kitchen table, eating lamb. Letting me sip his *retsina*. He, who made me one with my own six-year-old shadow. As I turned from the sun-spots of yet another incarnation locking me into a body. George Avgerinos, filling me with you, Bucephalus. Your massive black haunches. Flailing hooves strong as bronze breastplates. That white star blazing your forehead.

How that boy-turned-man wept at your war wounds. Burying you after the Battle of Hydaspes. Naming a city built over your glorious bones.

To sleep. Soundly. *In* those bones.
            As I learned the weeping. And the weeping learned me.

Your black coat. Large white star on your brow.
            Even your one piercing walleye.

How did my grandfather know I needed to ride both you *and* your shadow? That I needed coaxing to look into the sun, full-faced, sparing my shy, newly formed body the dark places within?

Not Pegasus and his wingèd seed. Not the belly of something
            wooden. On wheels. Waiting within the city to pounce.

But your massive flanks. Hoof-beat in sand. Wild, rearing, whinnying carving figure eights into the wind. Your proud

trumpet prance at dawn. Conquering Egypt. Babylon. Asia
Minor. Persia. Bactria.

                                  All the way to India.

Merging sun and   shadow. Moon and   sleep.
    Soundly. Within both yours and Alexander's bones.

As I entered the realm of being Greek. Feeling my clumsy
human body grow into something tender yet strong enough to
stand the burning sand. To absorb the dark marks I stared into
the sun. To carry phalanxes and generals miles in my wake,
within me, into the then-unknown blur of men that this boy,
freshly human, was about to become.

How Our Bones Refuse to Close

for my parents

This is how I love them. How I love
the world. This, how the world sees me.
Yes, there were eel ecstasies in mud,

migration habits of seahorse and wind
in the watery maps of my hands.
Sea coral from the Ionian. From the Aegean.

This scrape and that from reefs in the sea-sunk
ground as two lovers, twenty-four and twenty-two,
touched tongues, feeling the electrical tug

of deep places. And were born unto me.
I was born under a good sign, celestial drift
and belly-blur of the stars. I was born under

St. George and his horse. His white horse. There,
in the canary grass in the chest cavity of a dead crow.
The *yin* and *yang* of acacia leaves. Cypress beards.

A bowl of *avgolemono* soup. This is how I love.
This is how I shape a world. How my bones
open and clothe, keeping me from the hurt

places of the flesh. This is how families are born
into one another. *My* family. And our bones know. Our bones
refuse to close. There are holes in my bones. Minnow

shoals passing through me. Dolphin sound. Whale song.
Great migrations from starlight into womb water
where the blow hole says air and sea might finally be

enough. This is how I speak. How I *grow* my bones.
Grateful for the fluids of your flesh that made my flesh.
Even as you sink now into the ground, my father.

Even as your dust, mother, is burnt bone-blur
in a bag. O Bill. O Georgina. Your names still pass through
me. The sound of your voice. Eel ecstasies engendering

the mud. Migration habits of all my hands
might map. Follow the lines this way to the man's morning
shadow. Follow the lines that way to the gentle of her

touch. And so, minnow holes in our bones. And so starlight
in the mouth. And so St. George and his horse. And seahorses
releasing milky eggs in a cloud of could be and can't.

Settling the coral. The stones. Like a net of underwater stars.
A zodiac of words bleary and blurred. How can we ever truly
tell tone textures of the tongue, torn as we are from sound?

How can we word-blur and stir? Our bones, my parents—
open and clothed—grow, and we know the length
of one another. In the Ionian. The Aegean. Even the Chicago

River where we deepen the depths and dolphin-cry our names.
Though you are no longer in the body, your bones refuse
to close. The broken, the whole. This is how I love you.

This is how the world. The flood lamps our words lantern-cast
to reach. We minnow-merge into one another and through.
Still. Your voice, my voice, and starlight in the deeps.

Helen Avgerinos

1907–1996

You were my one grandparent, Nana, not born
in Greece. You could cook Greek food
better than anyone. *Moussaka. Pastitsio. Dolmades.*
I loved them all. Especially your *avgolemono* soup—
that froth of egg, lemon, and rice.

But your life was not all cooking. We lived
together when my mother's twenty-eight-year-old
unsure self walked back into your home
with her two boys. I was happy there with Nono's tales
of Zakynthos and with my two mothers. There were no words
back then for *joint custody* or *every other weekend*
at Dad's. Such a cleave was uncommon.
Like the stench of a rotten onion exposed
on the cutting board. Both halves needing to be
rinsed and thrown away.

                    But this is not about that.
It is about how you held yourself, Nana, even as you tore apart
the week-old Wonder Bread, placing it
on a day-old towel-wiped paper plate, telling me
to take it out front of the kitchen
picture window as a gift for the birds.

And they'd scatter when I pumped the screen door handle
with all the clumsiness of a six-year-old getting used
to being in a body again. Then I'd return with the plate

when I tossed the bread to the wind.
You taught me how to name things by color
streaks on a wing, the tilt of a beak, the way
certain birds would preen and seemingly fret over lost
tufts. Encouraged my annoyance with the squirrels
who'd dart in and steal our offering
from the flickers, woodpeckers, and jays.
To love the sound of pine needles in wind. Freezing rain
against the propane tank. Even the presence of garter snakes
you assured me lurked in our yard only for good.

Nono taught me the myths of Sparta
and Troy. *Aesop's Fables* and the sayings of Socrates.
The conquests of Alexander. Promised
that being Greek had already launched me
on an odyssey of unencumbered exploration. Where
navigation by stars was a way of grasping constellations
in the uncharted waters of my chest.
But you taught me to see the animals
we wept—landlocked as we were in Indiana—
and how the animals wept *us*.

And the sun rose most evenings inside
the moon. And the moon slept inside a burning
summer morning blossom, a blistering winter, an autumn
or spring when things withered and bloomed.
And *Nono* and *Nana* shared half
of the four corners of the letters
of their names. With the consonants
constant, only the vowels slightly askew.

You could cook and cook and cook. Roast lamb.
Pheasant stew. *Skordalia*—those puréed potatoes

gobbed with garlic so abundant the house literally reeked
for a week. That medicinal garlic drove away the odor
of any torn thing. And we moved our human bodies
like the sun and moon, our woods' swamp and the trees,
wind warbling through the hollow-boned
bodies of what we fed most days, even in winter.
When you'd send me out with the broken bread
of what I did not know was an offering of what was broken
inside me. As I tried to fill my newly human
body and give the fragments
of myself splintered in the cleaving
to be eaten and made whole.
Where I would go into the backyard
and bring the bread and break open
again and again.

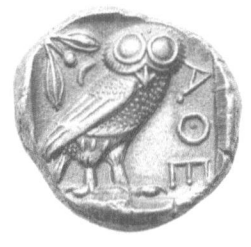

FIVE

The Grammar of the Body

On E. Ch. Gonatas and the Origin of
the Mirrors of Our Being

She had hanged tiny mirrors on trees for the birds to
look at themselves.
          —Epameinondas Ch. Gonatas

Here we go again, trying to see ourselves.

Let's say there is a forest raised on wolves' blood.

Let's pretend the lightning loves us. That we will burn forever.

Let's promise our mouths that we will one day speak without
speaking. That our insides will remain inside.

That Lautréamont's sewing machine and umbrella never met
on the dissecting table but in the copper gutters of our throats.

E. Ch. Gonatas knew this. Knew enough to avoid dust from
the sirocco coming in across the sea. Knew that it did not
originate from tropical air masses, as he'd been told, but from
abrasions inside animal dung fueling fires in the Sahara.

Yes, in the early days, he often met with Embirikos. With
Hatzilazarou. With Engonopoulos. Elytis. Gatsos. Sahtouris.
Kaknavatos.

Of course, he founded *Primal Matter* with Papaditsas in '58.
Splitting open a pomegranate sizzling throughout our blood.

Who in their right mind requires more than one name? Gonatas
thought.

Even each of the Nine Muses stood solitary. Bemused.

There is one speck of fire. One confused botfly in the horse's nostril.

Life could be beautiful, he thought, *as the fortuitous meeting of a botfly and hemostat in the silky underarm hair of the Belovèd.*

Lautréamont, Gonatas knew, would be pleased.

Might beg the birds to peer into the tiny mirrors they took as one another's mouths.

There is no point in saying it right.

We must persist in saying it right.

How could Gonatas have largely been forgotten? His poems stranded in a ditch in a mixture of broken branches, possum blood, and road salt?

The origins of how it all ends lie in *The Book of Perfect Eternity.*

Seeketh the advice on pages 109–113 in a one hundred-eight-page book.

Sometimes even letters and numbers mix, in a confusion of mouths. Stunted mirrors buried inside the bodies of birds.

That with which we speak flies into the kerosene lamps and singes letters of the word *mouths* off into *moths.*

Brother-my-sister. Say *no* when you mean *yes.*

Say *E. Ch. Gonatas* when you mean *Epameinondas Ch. Gonatas*.

Blur the names of the Muses as you might bend the night
bones breaking during the turbulent winds of sleep.

I say *Thalia*, Muse of pantomime and pastoral pain, when I
mean *Clio*, Muse of history and dead horse bones.

I say *Calliope*, Muse of epic agonies, when I mean *Urania*,
Muse of astronomy and the belly-burn of stars.

I say *Polyhymnia* when I am speechless in a forest of wolves'
blood. Amidst wind-ripping. In a moment of startled
lightning. When at last I reach the Sacred Word inside my
own saliva.

How could one so primal be tossed to the trees?

Dear Gonatas. E. Ch. Gonatas. Belovèd Epameinondas
Ch. Gonatas. You are here and not here. There and somewhere
swirling in the mouths of the other four Muses—Erato,
Euterpe, Melpomene, and Terpsichore.

Yes, "The Autopsy." Elytis closes my favorite poem of his with,
We shall have early fruit this year.

And I repeat it. Plant it here, again. In you, Gonatas. In the
mirrors of your mouth. In termite eggs you laid for us in
mounds far away, which are very close. In the bones of our
head as we lie sleeping, awake. Revoking our wrong. Thinking
our dream of you and the marvelous moist of your words was
only as slippery as smoke and could only last so long.

The Death of Kiki Dimoula

Poetry can make absence into presence. I call on the dead.
I invoke death.
            —Kiki Dimoula

They said it was a heart attack that came
for her. But it was her poems, backsliding
up into her throat, Kiki's throat, as she lay
in that hospital bed in Athens. She
who spent years of seaweed and sea lice
invoking the death of water, air, fire.
Even the earth rose up in one final push
to claim her words and draw them back down
into the soil from which they had come.

There was an icon of the Blessèd Virgin—
Panagia—above her bed. A startled weeping
as the paint came alive, the gold inlay,
more so when Kiki died. Like the filling
from a tooth. Flakes of wind, say, from the shimmering
olives, back unto the poet's throat. Church bells
rang their muted, muddled selves. And the sea
seemed to weep, though only the Aegean
knew the origin of its salts—whether
the water arose from the sea bottoms
roiling beneath the waves or from long nights
of tears in the complex caves of the body,
so long abandoned beneath the brass lamps.

I call on the dead, she said. *I invoke death*,
saying so, even when she could no longer speak.

Even as she struggled those final hours
beneath an icon of all that was holy
and all that could be a poem, if it gave its gold
back unto the mouth of the poet
who lay there, before it, with an open throat,
waiting to be filled. With death.

Thusness / Dhimitris Dhoukaris Contemplates
   the Grammar of the Body

Thus, he spoke "Pythia's Words." "The Sarcophagus."
Even "The Grammar of the Body."

Thus, when the fire came all the way from Morocco,
there was a cooling rain inside his Leftist skull.

This, Dhimitris Dhoukaris remembered from breadlines.
From the Civil War. A dream dreaming itself partial and torn.

Sure, there was a pheasant on fire in his chest.
Mice bone cracked whenever he breathed too vigorously.

And when the wind came, all the leaves, oddly, calmed down.
Please, he insisted, *I only love the act of political forgiveness.*

Complete political forgiveness. Here, taste my tongue.
By which he meant, *If in the time of sorrow.*

Which sounded like, *In the beginning was the Word.*
Which very much resembled, *Hey you, come here!*

Dhimitris Dhoukaris composed all his poems on a boat.
He sailed from here to there, but only in the mud of his mind.

All of this added up to being born with the dual
disposition of a Gemini. To dying within the constellation

of Aires. The god of war. All of this could be said
to replenish himself. And how his three and a half years

in prisons, in detention camps, continued
to hurt. Thus, he spoke "Pythia's Words."

The High Priestess. Where she sat in the Temple of Apollo.
At the Holy Omphalos. And teetered on a tripod cauldron

over a chasm the size of what eats people
from inside. The answers that rose up

through her resembled maps. A map of war-torn Greece.
A map of a pockmarked face. A face insisting stars had burned

their divisions into it. *Where there is a sarcophagus,
we have "The Grammar of the Body."* Thus, he said such things.

Thus, such things also said *him*. And the world
turned as if the war years were topsoil. And the cooling

rain in his skull actually camped in his throat.
And his throat spoke tones of maybe, mostly,

and herewith. *Dear Friend. Dear The-Moon-Dropping-Its-Doe-
Heavy-Self.* Thus, Dhimitris Dhoukaris remembered moonlight

on the Acropolis. Moonlight in a grove. He remembered
whiskey and Cavafy. And the canebrake of Akutagawa.

Alexandria kept being Alexandria. Kyoto, Kyoto. Far away
yet within reach. Even death squads in Athens seemed close.

Thus, a dream was dreaming itself partial and torn.
Thus, a dream was dreaming itself partial in the partially torn.

Paul Delvaux Dreams That His Dream of Perfect Women with Classically Sculpted Beauty Is Not a Dream at All

based on Delvaux's painting The Lamps, *1937*

The perfect breast, suggested, half-hidden
by an arm. Gorgeous step forward
and moonlit hips. The burning

inside glass. Regulated by some touch or other
to flare or dim the wicks of disembodied lamps.
What are they moving toward, these women,

these epitomes of earth's drenching
dark? Each sculpted form, left leg lifting
forward into—what? Yes, the classical Greek

colonnade is just out of reach. Dark mounds
of earth rise behind these women, as if a mirror
of dimming milk. As if the near-empty plains

in which they reside hide corpses from inside
their own beautiful core. What battle, what war lasting
ten terrible years, are these women fleeing? Coming

into? This could be the death plains of Sparta. Or
the 295 sea miles to besiege the city of Troy,
into which all beauty steps as it moves toward origin.

All for a Helen, Seferis wrote. The way forward, Delvaux knew,
is the way back into frozen perfection. Thawing. But not
moving. How they loved him, these women

he could create, not only in body but in their undying
affection. For him. Delvaux. For the brushstrokes inside
the turbulent tides of his mind. As if standing in front

of their dimming calm. He could embrace a mirror
that made him temporarily whole. How they hated him.
Each replicating one another. With their blank stares. Their

free-me-from-this-body look. If hate was possible.
Their unmovable bodies. Locked, as they were,
into the place he chose to display and gaze long

upon their form. Why place them mid-stride
against a lamp? What part of their beauty burned
inside him, already dimming into the moon-

trenched night? *This is why the world
is such an empty place*, Delvaux mused,
as he brushstroked these women

over and again into Aphrodite. Hera. Hestia.
Even Circe. He feared the pig he might become,
tied—as he was—to the creaking mast

of his paintbrush. The lust and hull of his canvas. Depths
of gesso for this hip or that. *All for a Helen*, he thought.
And he moved into them, entering these women

with achy grays, anemic greens—colors he imagined their inner
worlds to be. Only sounds of dark could embrace the dimming
that fed them and their incessant lamps, fires inside them

that Paul Delvaux—lonely as he was—hoped to one day seize.

Giorgos Vakalo Paints Egypt
Without Even Knowing He Has

There is an octopus extending itself
throughout the world. Shaped like a sunken moon

among the wavering, watery reeds. Someone
is calling from my past. As if dialing the sore places

inside. Inside them or inside me remains uncertain.
Look at it this way. The world keeps falling apart.

Look at it again, and 6,000 people died of Covid
just yesterday in India alone. Some say disease is

dis-ease. Giorgos Vakalo's colors calm the night.
Even when it is not night. Did the horses burn?

The barn stampede? Is that a half moon in the painting
or a patch of gauzy night eclipsing the sun's sun? Either way,

things move toward one another and shake loose.
I wish I could reach out, touch his hand, light Vakalo's

cigarette, assure him he is not dead, that even though
he is gone, his brushstrokes retain. An octopus

or an octagon? A watery reed culling my name. Giorgos
Kalamaras or Giorgos Vakalo? Inside the wind, the sirocco

brings fragments of what could have been. Long-buried
across the sea in the blowing sands and graves weeping

for us. The tombs, the hecatombs, we could never quite reach.

Vowel in the Mouth: The Baptism of Eleni Vakalo

She was said
to have been born
        with a vowel in her mouth

And during her
baptism into the Holy Faith
        she was dunked three times

into a Magritte painting
the one with the horse and rider
        blurring into trees

Vowel in the mouth
submerged into the baptismal font
        one two three times

There was no pause perhaps
a little but not a momentous pause
        and so her poems often

avoided commas
as, if, a, great, wind, rose,
        slowly, inside her, night

belly—this Eleni Vakalo
was grateful for
        just as she adored the paintings

of her late husband Giorgos
who seemed somehow to paint
   much of what was inside her

even before they met
She wrote nine volumes
   of art history and theory

all nine together easily
divisible by three
   Three times three equaled

The City of Nine Gates
the nine openings of the body
   to be controlled she'd read about

in the Hindu *Upanishads*
The Face of Post-War Art in Greece
   she said when that volume appeared,

and, the, entire, body,
of, the, dead, had, to, stop, and, listen
   Then she wrote about

Paul Delvaux his classical
influences even as his multiplied brides
   seemed to keep replicating

not only themselves something inside
Delvaux that he had lost like the word *but*
   We are always losing that

which we have
not yet fully grasped
            and only when it flies out

of our mouths
like bees searching their bloodlines
            do we finally understand

the great migrations back to tomorrow
Such thoughts she wrote she
            taught us especially when she

herself departed for Olympus
and the rain in our mouths
            rose up rather than fell

that day to feed the ground
O Eleni there are times
            when we finally understand

what. It. Means. To. Stop.
And. Listen. I am so tired
            of telling people my mouth

telling them to comb their hair
while studying their shoulder-length
            strength in the death

of Delilah's younger sister
who happened to be
            a most gentle she-wolf

In other words
I truly love the vowel
            that passed from your mouth

into the owl
impersonating a cypress branch
            In other words it is good

very good to be dipped three times
into the open body
            of a wood pigeon and blessed with its blood

We somehow learn
to forgive the mouse
            its fear of sudden flying

grasped in the talons
of midnight disguised
            as a locomotive pouring out

of a brick fireplace
in Magritte's *Time Transfixed*
            When we're baptized

in the paintings of one
who so loved the world
            When we read the poems

the poems of you Eleni Vakalo
the poet who wrote poems
            If we listen closely we can hear

the sudden churning of fire
and smell the rubble smoke and steam
               in how we displace one brick

after another in tracking
the contents of our core—one brick
               at a time Eleni from your

most astute and studied mouth

Alexandros Panagoulis Weighs the World
One Word at a Time

Count the rat turds in your food, Alexandros,
and you can notch the calendar with another sun-sunken

moon. You wrote your poems on the walls of your jail cell,
sometimes with your own blood. It is difficult for me

with my air conditioning, shelves of books, and full belly
to completely grasp that writing with your blood is not

a metaphor. I weigh the world one word at a time. I weigh
the world of the literal and the bee swarm in my mouth.

It is like, I begin to say to you. And then I stop,
gutted with guilt for your years of actual blood

and walls. Tell me, what is it like to be the sea
inside the sea? To be the strength of the current

preventing you from swimming to your comrades
waiting in the boat after you tried to kill the coup?

You could not swim strongly enough. The Colonels put you
in that place of assassination. I see the walls and say *walls*.

I see walls and say *trees bending away from the fire in your mouth.*
I cut a finger while carving a carrot and say *blood of my blood.*

I read your poems and ask what you coughed up upon
your cot before the Angel of Amnesty arrived? What finger

did you use to soak your grief forever into concrete?

The Death of Konstandinos Karyotakis Reborn in the Birth-Blood Poems of Dinos Siotis

after Dinos Siotis's "Why You Would Have Committed Suicide Again If You Were Living Today O Konstandinos Karyotakis!"

Death is a deep-frozen bird thawed in the poet's mouth.
Death is Wire Press and barbed fencing inside bodies of birds.

Death is a poem stalking the poet's limp.
Death is an Armenian apple in the Greek poet's mouth.

Death is the man asking for beer and a pack of Zante Filters.
Death is Olga. And Rita. And Mando Aravantinou.

Death is Seferis and his incurable wound.
Death is Maria and Konstandinos sharing three cookies a day.

Death is the promise of the reincarnation of every stone.
Death is the Trojan Horse alive with swords, clubs, and spears.

Death is Troy, sleeping off a long night of lamb and wine.
Death is a quietly lit torch lighting the cobblestone way.

Death is syphilis, incurable at the time of a 1928 suicide.
Death is a gunshot in the heart of a man shamed into oblivion.

Death is Maria, her tuberculous cough caught in a photograph.
Death is how to tell his love that he could never share her bed.

Death is the dinner bowl, left out for unknown cats.
Death is a Blue Willow plate left out in the rain.

Death is a virus not yet agreeing to kill itself.
Death is the pandemonium of a pandemic pirating the mouth.

Death is a corpse wrapped in a tablecloth and napkins.
Death is the body risen on the third day from a cave.

Death is a prostitute resurrected in the body of a savior.
Death is *The Book of Books* learning how to read itself in trees.

Death is hyena scat dropped here into everywhere at once.
Death is how mice roam through the animal's slow bones.

Death is Konstandinos reborn on the island of Tinos in 1944.
Death is death risen in the blood-lit birth of Dinos Siotis.

Death is, *I am here, my brothers and sisters, in the groan of your bones.*
Death is how we are given a second chance. And a third.

Death is not death, Dinos seems to say, in anaphoric allure.
Death is not death, he repeats, into bodies swollen and disowned.

Triptych for Ritsos

In the time of the Colonels

The Sanctity

"And if they go to shoot you, remember,
keep your mouth shut," breathed the old man
leaning over him. "And careful to always
wear your thickest shirt, or the heat
from your belly will rush out
all at once and leave you
empty."

But Lefteris wasn't listening again. He sat
at the bar, deep in some other music—the amber
stirring of his whiskey, the secrets
of the glass only the coldness of the ice
knew—watching across the smoke a woman
watching him, stroking with her hands the lull
of her hair.

The moon's sigh poured across the bar, spilling
its sack of fine flour. Through the window,
he could see snow piling up, that drift
of vowel whose cart could carry him.

From the distance, a familiar breathing, a moist
trembling arose, close, as if from his own
skin, like a life he could not prove,
like the scent of his mother's voice
he carried. Still.

Tonight, he thought, in the flesh of some absolute
sound, he could die, perfectly.

Dusk

*There is only one woman left in the world, and she has
died.* This, Lefteris thought as he found himself that night
kneeling among ferns that swayed in a garden of dusk, her soil
restless and clinging. The shadows of pines crept low on the
hill, moving into him, the way memory enters, a moment,
that distance within an embrace. He could hear ants bend
through growing rings of tree-breath, orbits of moonlight in
the velvety bark. A wind of starlight nuzzled the pores on the
back of his left hand, becoming the emptiness near form. In a
damp room a doctor hovered near the pale light of the waiting
corpse. What had been lost pulsed in the plants breathing water
into him. *There is only one body*, he thought, *and she is lost,
waiting in the grass, near the beating star. One woman dying. One
star that sinks into layers of water ferns thirst for.*

Closing the Parentheses

"But where has he gone? I miss him,"
the butcher was saying. "Where *is* Lefteris?"
It was a woman he did not recognize, who turned
in his shop slightly, shifting her gaze near
the open window. Her voice, like the sound of starlight
in the ears of the deaf, became the lilacs' mist
of bees moving through the butcher—

"Look for him, friend, very near the end
of every sentence you speak, where olives breathe
through wormwood and wind
hollows, in the distance
exhaling from the heat
in a woman's strong arms
and opening inside
a boy's body, in closing
hours of candlelight
soaking near the gritty bottom
a cup of cold coffee meditates on.

"There was a man who loved
the world so much, he died
from it, from lying awake hours each night
drinking starlight through the dark spot
on his forehead. There was a man
who slept close to his life, clinging
to what he hoped he spoke
with his skin.

"Look for him further, inside
the well's restless water,
inside the swelling
pores that rise
in an arm's lift,
in the scent of a passing
moon darkening the reach
between the train's tracks,
near the limp in an old woman's
rainy street, in swirls
of mysterious hair
steaming beneath a streetlight's
final breath."

Mikis Theodorakis Contemplates the Rise and Fall of the World

It was a cypress or a willow. He lifted himself into the tree
as a child and heard a piece of perfect music.

Lately, his liver keeps telling him to cleanse the world
with a word. Lately, he sets human suffering to song.

And the wind foraging his mouth makes its way
into back alleys and coffee shops, pharmacies and free

clinics, searching for the proletariat. Birds sound
like Dmitri Shostakovich awarding him the 1957 Gold Medal

at the Moscow Music Festival. How can then be now?
The years keep bringing poverty and loss. Once, he lay

on a beach, with Anthony Quinn and Irene Papas, composing
the theme to *Zorba the Greek* in ways the sea and its stormy

foam told. When he climbed trees he heard Greek folk music
and the Byzantine Liturgy both. How to forget? How to forget

being arrested during the Civil War, deported to Makronisos?
He tells his grandchildren to listen to the wind when the rain

falls. To light a fire and read the poems of Ritsos only when
the embers sink. To give a slice of water, a cup of bread,

to the poor. They don't believe him and grind their teeth
when he tells of how he had been buried. Buried alive. Twice.

His throat stuffed with dirt. His music left for dead.

Yannis Kondos Wakes One Morning to Discover His Throat Has Closed Shut

Eelgrass and something like insects
in his ear. God help him reading Dickens

midnights while watching Luis Buñuel
films. The Cape of Good Hope was just

a fantasy, he knew, as he tried to unstuff
his ears. His mouth. Yes, the throat. The marigold

throat he knew he deserved. *Plant a kiss here,*
he told the unknown woman

he passed on a rain-soaked street, pointing
to his Adam's apple. He knew his poems

were full of irony. Or was it *ironing?*
The wrinkled shirt. Disheveled pants.

The unpolished shoe. Wait!
If he took a hot iron

to his shoe he might burn
right through to the foot

that could carry him away
from Greek Military Rule

and bring him home safely
to the town of Aigio. How to kill

the myth while *living* the myth? Look
into the eyes of Medusa and turn

into the everlasting light
of sugar? Kill the throat while *speaking*

the throat? He looked in the mirror,
heard the disenchantment

of Ritsos. Of the would-be
assassin, Alexandros Panagoulis.

He considered a bee colony
as one way to hold his throat. Closed.

He pissed against a cypress tree
down into its roots, gingerly,

while trying to sing, once again,
straining the names of the Colonels

as if they were just friends with whom
he had only had a minor quarrel.

Hymns of the Body of Mando Aravantinou

(So we inhabit, the aged and wise hymnographer and I,
the outskirts of the nameless town.)
—Mando Aravantinou

So there are hymns of the body and hymns of fire.

Mando Aravantinou gave her body unto the lightning in her mouth.

Love is like that. And so is starlight. And so is garlic in the mouths of the dead.

Mando exhausted every pronoun. Denunciation. Deceit. Disappearance.

The Colonels, she said, *are flecks of inept tornado resin.*

By which she meant, *Yes, the fact of my father-invocation disturbed the growth of trees.*

By which she meant, *Height of the emergent linguistic achievement is a cold sore on the mouth.*

By which she emphasized, *Seferis was right: "Wherever I travel Greece wounds me."*

So there are hymns of the sacred and hymns of the profane.

Anthropologies of the dead.

A dissected rooster at the Bureau of Surrealist Research
revealing an undigested lobster in its bowels.

And the hymnographer offers praise with hymns *unto* his hymns.

The chronology of her words, Mando's words, upon the
Grammar of the Greeks.

The meaning of memory and all it forgets.

Everything takes place in complete silence and precision, she said.

Exploratory beards. And men with sudden mustaches hiding
fragments of all they have scattered in their military stance.

Hymns of the body, she said, standing there, all aglow with
lightning. *Hymns of fire. The almost-word in the almost-said.
The almost-word restless in the everlasting mouths of the dead.*

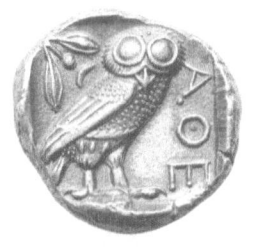

SIX

For My Family

Panagia

Panagia means the All-Holy or the Most Holy. The standard Western Christian designation of "St. Mary" is rarely used in the Orthodox East, as Mary is considered the holiest of all human beings and therefore of higher status than the Saints.

Delvaux prayed   to your birthmark, Belovèd,
that mole   hidden in your left   armpit
that it—that *you*—could make   each of his women
                              most holy.
Which is what *Panagia* means.   As did Giorgos Vakalo,
painting underwater   seascapes, amoeba-like,
fluid   as the female moon.

They say Stalin prayed   to you, too. He clothed
the churches,   asking—superstitiously—that you not
strike him   dead. That the womb-domes
of Orthodoxy   no longer hold your image.
Of course,   Georgios Papadopoulos
begged your forgiveness   with each   execution
of a left-wing   dissident.   Even during the Reign
of the Colonels   when he made it unlawful in Greece
not to be religious.

                    O Panagia. O   Most Holy.
How many nights as a child   I prayed to grow up
          into a hero like Odysseus   to enter Troy
disguised in a   horse   and try to rescue   Helen.

I prayed, prayed   to you   for a tree

fort to bless the shagbark hickory   that led to the swamp.
I prayed for snow days from school.   I prayed for a hound
dog to scour   the woods with me. Prayed   for the mulberry
stains on my jeans   to disappear   so as not
to upset my mother's $1.35 an   hour   checking
groceries   at Hi-Lo in Highland.
Prayed for the ant I named *Georgie*   and killed—
by mistake—when I was six,   thinking we were playing.

Now the train whistle cries   through me, through
the long   night. And in the dark,   the dark
approaches more   dark and   darkly moves
its dimming hours   into me. No longer
Orthodox, I keep still your icon   tucked in a chest
of drawers,   lovingly covered   with a silk
meditation cloth from an ashram   in India,
decades after the image hung   on my childhood wall.
Papou and *Yia-Yia*   brought your icon to my baby-self,
from Greek Town on Halsted. Their names   signed,
dated on masking tape still clinging   to its back.
Dedicated, of course, to   *Georgie*.

To whom did they intend?   Their newborn
grandson? The ant   I would soon kill
by giving it   my name? My future
ant-bitten self   sunk,   still, in regret
for its tiny twitching   body? Or the holes   I forgot
to put into its container.   Those most holy gaps
my mouth   still makes   somehow
replaying   its death rain-soaked   days
or in the midnight   depth   of my poems?
Is that why   I recognized the Jains,   the yogis,
the Buddhist monks—their regard   for every sentient
being—when at sixteen   I pledged my life?

114

Yes, Delvaux must have   prayed to you   with each stroke
of his brush.   And Stalin,   fearing you. And Papadopoulos
executing what he knew   you most loved.
Yes, *Papou* and *Yia-Yia* gave me   your icon. Gave me
what I imagine   is your most hidden   mole
                        in a most secret place.
A darkness that will never   blemish and only embrace.

And *Papou's* grandfather—my great-great-grandfather—
Panagiotis Kalamaras, named   for you, Panagia. As is
Yia-Yia's father,   my great-grandfather Panayiotis
Demopoulos. Up and down   my family
tree,   many men received your womanly Word
                        and its seed.

O Panagia. O gorgeous   gap   in my throat.
When I come across you   in my drawer—you,
the *All-Holy*—   I still close my eyes and kiss you.
All that inner bowing brought forth   into my third   eye.

Bread and wine,   wine and the sluicey juice
of the grape, they say,   miraculously becomes the Body
and the Blood. I place   my lips upon your feet.
Kiss those who have come before   me
out of the thick salt air   and donkey bray
in Pharaklatha.   Zakynthos.   Solaki.
Somehow manifesting in masking tape   in the writing
of my grandparents   sixty-seven years on your back.
Giving me, still—without knowing—   their olives
and their leaves.   And the silver breeze that might
relieve my   weeping. Calm the twitching insect   deaths
inside me. With their Greek language and   their seed.
Giving me their mountains,   the body and blood
                        of their sea.

Photo of Young Love: George Avgerinos and Helen Bennett in the Backyard of Helen's Older Sister Grace, Chicago Heights, Illinois, *Circa* 1922

He has come a long way from his island in Greece
to this isle of grass in Chicago Heights.

Selling fruit in his grocery store when she first saw him
in the store window and brought her desire

for something sweet into his little shop.
Helen, he said, in broken English, after learning

her name, *I know you already*. My grandmother
looks stunned, sitting in the grass, leaning

into how good it feels to be loved. Which is also
his shoulder. The scent of his aftershave. Hairnet holding her

fifteen-year-old locks in place in the fashion of 1922.
They are so young, it hurts. They have barely touched

what it feels like to inhabit the earth
and beg of it its release. Nono's shoes are stylish,

laced as they are, as if he could anticipate
the long years together and the need to bind a love

that is only just now beginning a thread.
His dark hair holds, still, waves of the Ionian.

The same sea he dove into just six years before
from cliffs to gather fish after throwing dynamite

so their white bellies would rise to the surface.
Nana is sloe-eyed, shielding the sun, as if she knows

looking too hard into the brilliance of things
can only last so long. Within a year, they will marry.

They will love and touch and love
as if they were continually touching

spring. As if the lilacs, unseen behind them,
would temper years and inhabit any possible

pain. Earth rises up to meet them. And they oblige,
submerging themselves in the new grass, which they know

must be sprouting from within them. They are so young,
they cannot conceive their bodies aging. Arthritis. Parkinson's.

Nights without sleep. Death-moments they will want to kill.
They don't care if they get grass stains or chiggers.

Nono is even wearing white shirt and silk tie,
knowing it's best to look groomed

since his attempt at English marks him with his ten days
of crossing the Atlantic. Nana loves sipping the slow syllables.

His broken English somehow breaks something open inside
her. Something she knew was there but could never quite

reach. Nothing can compel her now not to love him.
It feels so good to love *love* itself. Nothing

can be reversed as these two giveth themselves
unto the grass that stirs in waves that mimic the undulations

of the sea. *Blessèd be the sea,* Nono must surely
be thinking. It brought him fish in Zakynthos

and saved his family from hunger. Now the grass, too,
must not be just an island, but the sea itself

in which George's and Helen's salt must mix.
How could they know, lost as they are

in youth, that their youngest daughter would one day marry
a man with a name derived from *calamari*—meaning *squid.*

How the squid of the Kalamaras blood
of their grandsons would swim back through

this sea-sound ground and embrace the *morning star*
from which the name *Avgerinos* descends. This moment,

elongated, opens so wide chiggers can't bite,
and the unseen lilacs bloom in each breath's release.

This breathing. Core. Locked, it seems, in a sister's backyard
in Chicago Heights is the grace Helen's sister Grace gives

them. Where a fifteen-year-old leans into a self she finds
in an eighteen-year-old shoulder, as if wrapped in a long

and lasting vowel. Coupled to youth that cannot see
beyond itself into a world of ocean, salt, and squid.

A world meshed with a moment of frozen light
in backyard spring, exposing dumb young so loving, it hurts.

Stelios Avgerinos

1880–1953

Let's say it's not just your blood that's in me, great-grandfather, but circles the barn swallow asserts mornings near the birdfeeder. Or the yellow angles of the grosbeak, the entirety of the sun contained inside the hollow bones of something that small.

Let's say the stories are wrong. That you and my great-grandmother—Angeline Peromalis—never took to the mountains of Zakynthos for a shoot-out with her disgruntled father and brothers before they agreed for you to wed.

That the vultures in that mountain crevice are not perched in my own blood.

That my blood is not perched in my mouth.

That my mouth is not thick with blankets of Ionian sea salt.

Lord knows you were a tough son of a bitch. That on the boat from Greece anyone who laughed at the way you stumbled through the syllables of *Chicago* was thereafter careful whenever they moved to the ship's rail and pissed in moonlight.

Let's say you didn't come to this country to quell the crush of pain. That all sins from the Old Country were forgiven. That the icon of St. Dan you carried all those miles long remained luminous in your red velvet bag with jackknife and *tsarouchi*—those hand-sewn moccasins worn mostly by the rural and "uncouth."

That the extra thumb on your right hand was not a deformity but a measure of reaching toward the unknown. Even into the astonishment of those who glimpsed it from time to time and believed that—though awake—they had not yet stirred from sleep.

Let's say we *don't* stir. That none of us stirs. That we too often sleep even as we work. That our daily toil—if done right—is our practice, our way one day out of these bodies into a world where the slow dark darkens the slowness we most need.

Stelios—belovèd great-grandfather Stylianos—it is cliché to say, *I wish we had met. That the years between us are thin.* Then I remember we *have* met—not just in my blood but in swirls of cigar smoke. In each fleck of sea salt on the skin of a toasted almond. In the dark pit of an olive. In the grapevines your son George, the grandfather with whom I grew up, cultivated in our backyard. In field recordings of *rembetika* from 1912 that I listen to many rain-soaked moons like tonight.

Yes, we have met—not just in my blood but through the impossible bodies of birds. In the hollow bones of this sparrow or that. This grosbeak or finch. Perhaps in an owl carving the dark with its screech of moonlight from the island of Zakynthos or from the Maumee, here in Indiana. Where it tends the dark places—swamp roots and their sinking. Minds the moon as it watches over remnants of sun dying in and out of the courtship of lightning bugs. Where in our daily work we, too, might crush the bones of a rabbit, raccoon, or mouse. And with the sun in our bellies (more, really, the

fading moon), we bathe most mornings in mud puddles of
rain-soaked leaves mixed with possum droppings and fur.
And—like you on the ship's bow looking miles of ocean west
toward America—with the dawn wind of the slow dark slowly
born into us.

With Sappho at the Grave of Angeline Avgerinos

1882–1940, born Angeline Peromalis

*And so, you must banish all thought
of wrist slashing, of keeping the fish's
long sad fin and donning only soft orange
or rum-gold robes*, Sappho said, clutching my hand,
guiding it across the lyre strings of her throat.

*There it is in your path. Quinsy—
that abscess that denied
the throat of your great-grandmother
Angeline.*

I stood with Sappho in the cemetery
in Steger, Illinois. Touched the rose
quartz cross that protects my great-grandmother's
grave. To die at age fifty-eight,
having never known the Second World War
or even how one city called Hiroshima
could, for decades, cloud
the rest of the world?

There was a taxidermy in my chest.
Quail flush, fifteen feet away,
from my grandfather George's hole.
Pheasant scent from his hunting years
whenever I heard my name in the switchgrass,
the same as his. When I heard its single syllable
drawn from the long, slow dark

of his bone. Wing-snap
when the three vowels
of Zakynthos somehow mouthed *grandfather*,
great-grandmother, when they boarded the boat
and left the Ionian together. Something resembling
the story of that medic
from Mysore sewing a tuberculous
peacock into the cavity
of a sadhu's collapsed chest.
Sending *that* body back to France
rather than that of René Daumal.

Who ultimately was fooled?
The village folk? The bird? The disease?
Bacteria in the lining of the lung?

> *And so,* Sappho spoke the voluptuous
> lyre strings of her throat, *you must banish*
> *the last star. Name it* Nagasaki. *Name it*
> Auschwitz. *Tongue it*
> *toward dissolve. Call it* Angeline.
> Stelios. Helen. Pericles and Stavroula.
> *Even* Miguel—*anything that resembles an olive*
> *root, in a jail cell, decomposing*
> *beneath the foot of Franco.*

To die, dear great-grandmother,
far from your island
having never heard
the words *computer chip* or *DVD* or
even *History Channel?*

There it was, like the Greek Resistance
cleaving to a cliff-face echoing dynamite
blast and donkey bray. Like René Daumal
and Miguel Hernández singing, still, at the edge
of becoming beautiful. Like quince
whose white flower quivers beneath
the hawthorn, shouting aromatic seeds
of applelike fruit for eight decades
up from her crabgrass
into the thicket: *Dearest great-grandson.*
Carry my cross, my rose-
colored stone. Call it
Giorgos; *call it* George. *Call it*
history of the world,
or no. *Call it live*
as a grosbeak—wing-struck
and stuck—in the certain salve
of your throat.

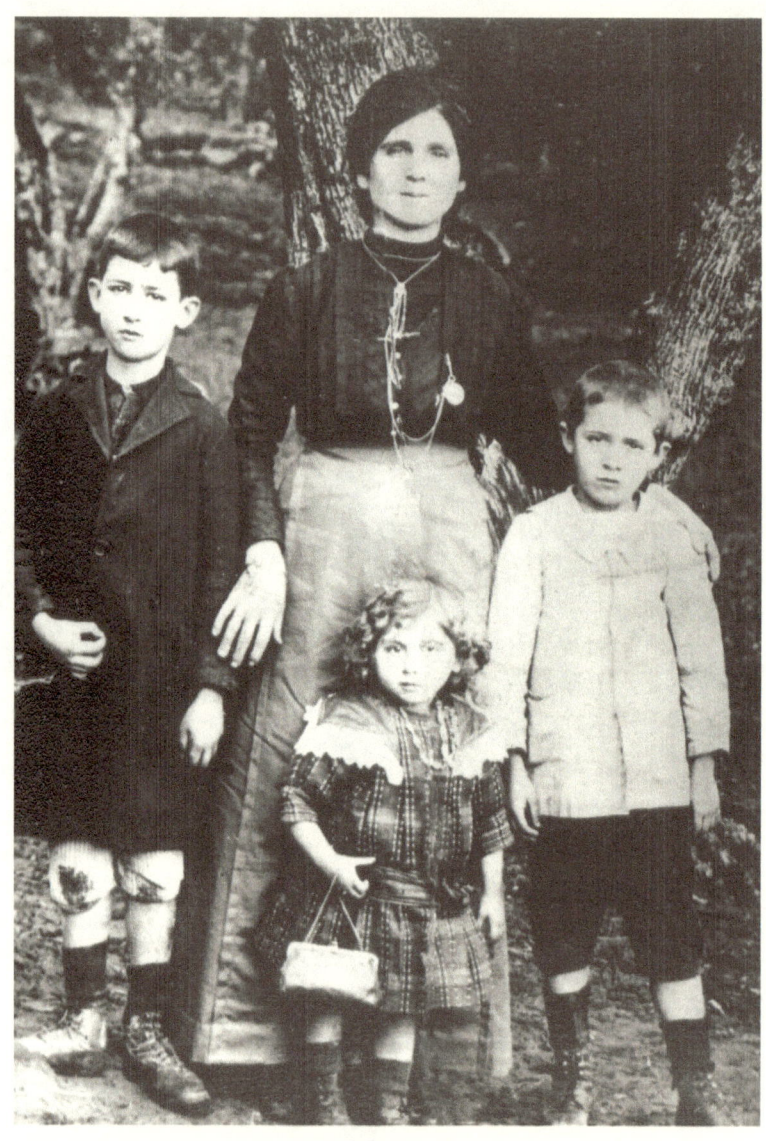

Angeline Avgerinos (George's maternal great-grandmother) and her three children (from left): George (George's grandfather), Martha, and Dan in Zakynthos, Greece, just prior to emigrating to the United States, *circa* 1916.

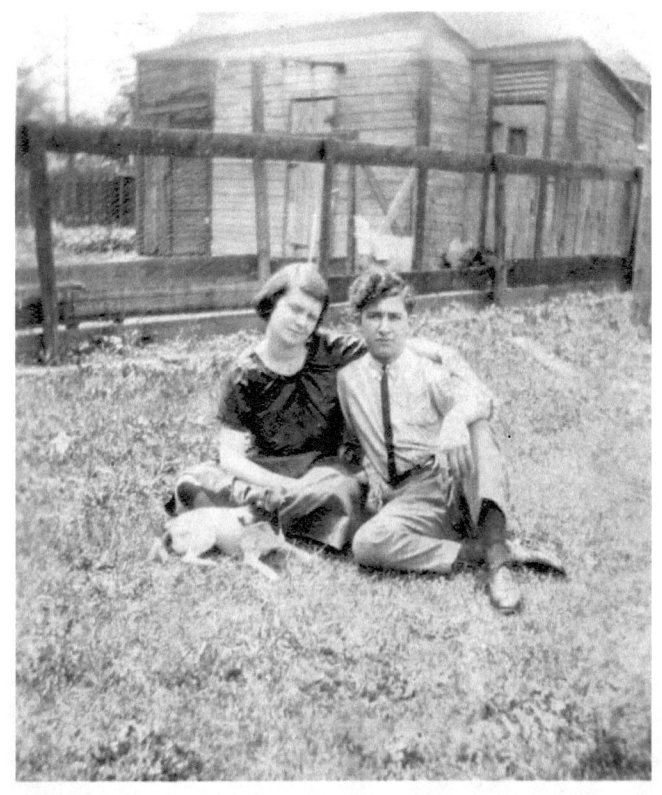

Helen and George Avgerinos (George's maternal grandparents) as a young couple prior to getting married, *circa* 1922.

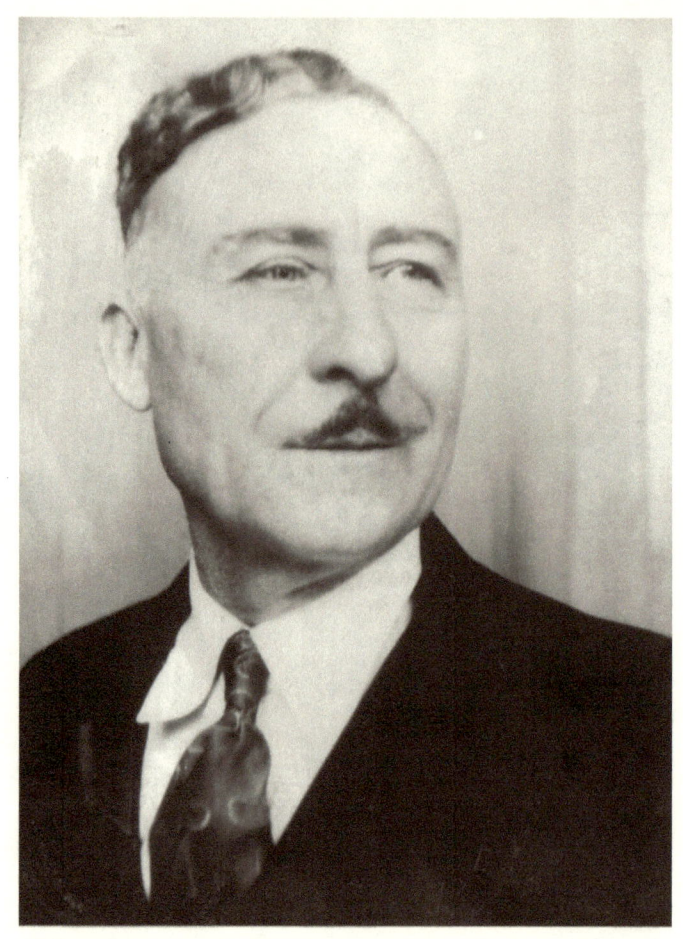

Stylianos (Stelios) Avgerinos (George's maternal great-grandfather).

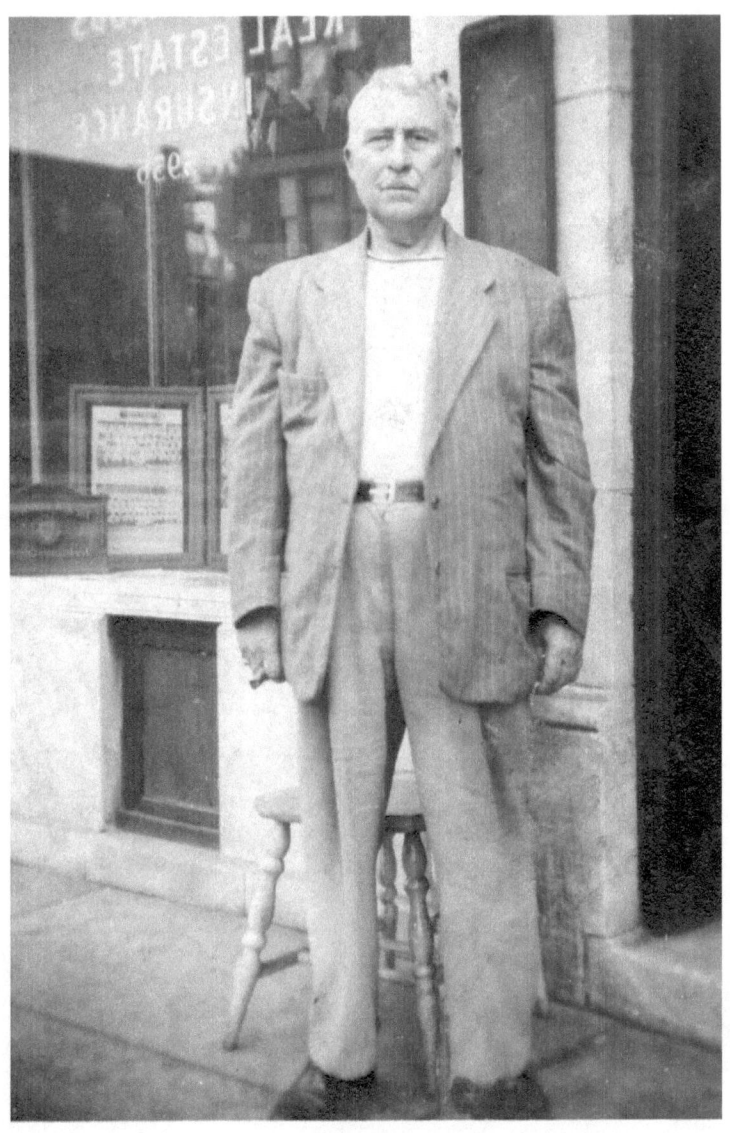

Stylianos (Stelios) Avgerinos.

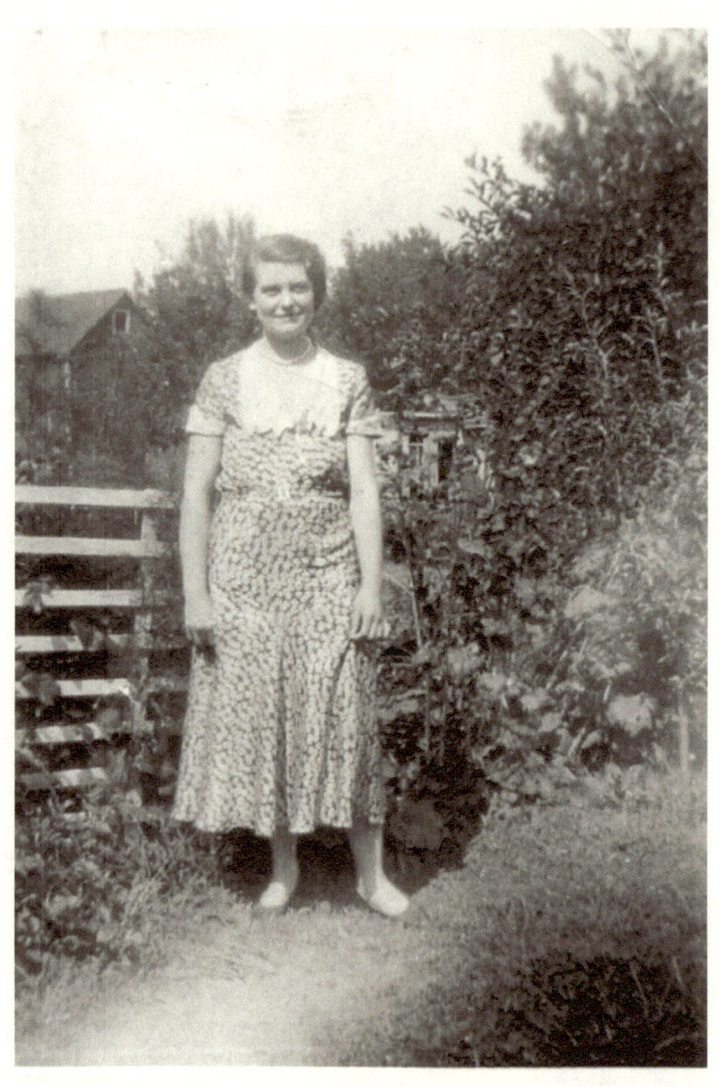

Helen Avgerinos (George's maternal grandmother), 1929.

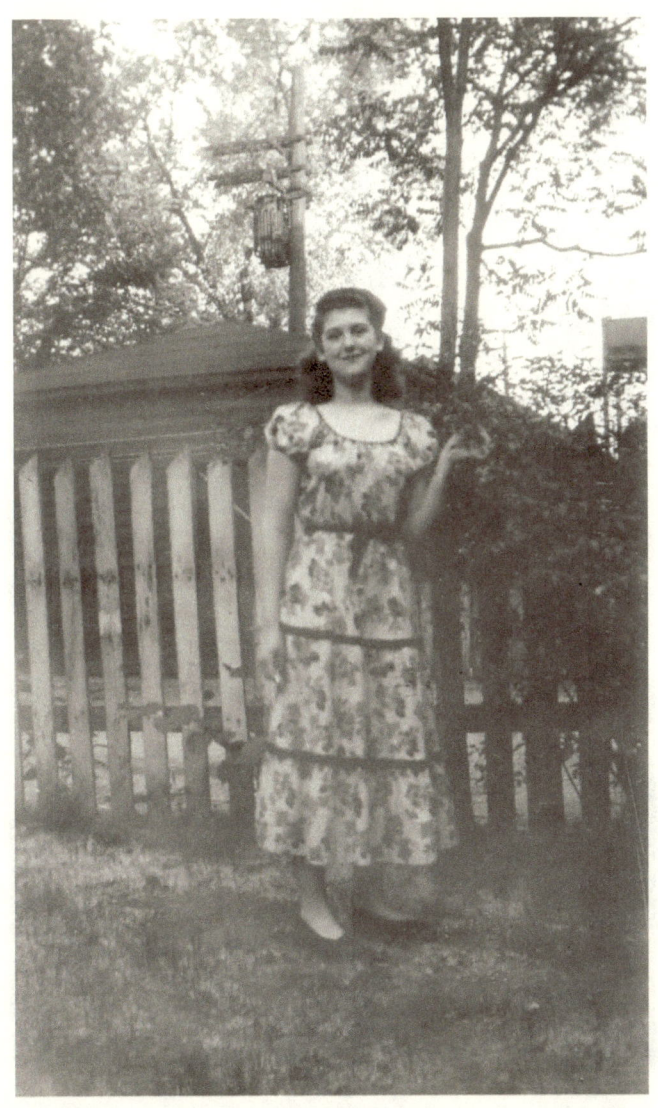

Georgina (Gina) Allen, née Avgerinos (George's mother).

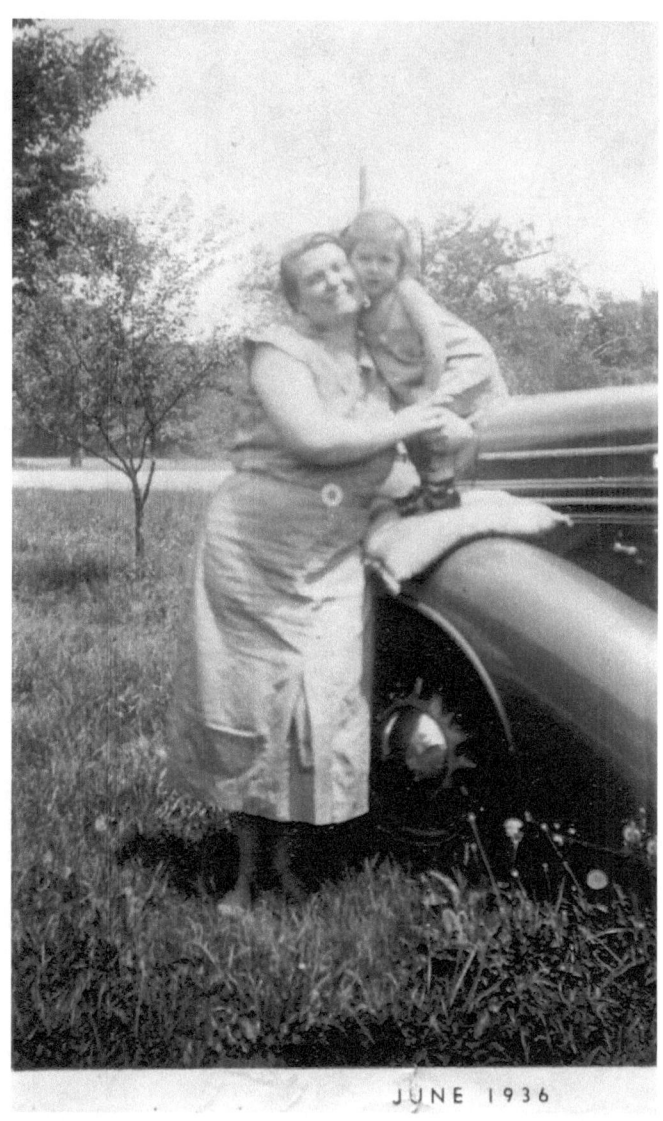

JUNE 1936

(Above and facing page): Helen Avgerinos and daughter Gina (with two unintentionally similar poses several years apart), 1936 and *circa* 1951.

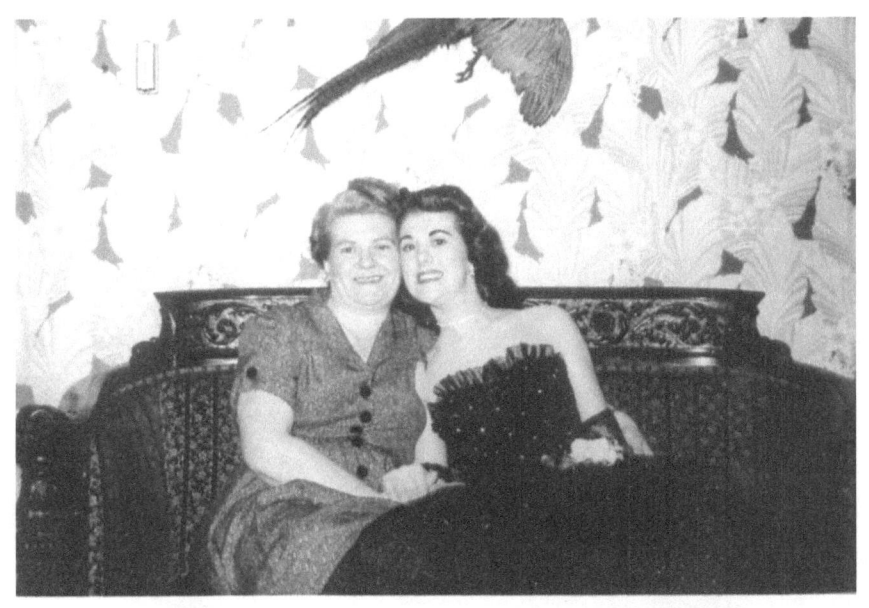

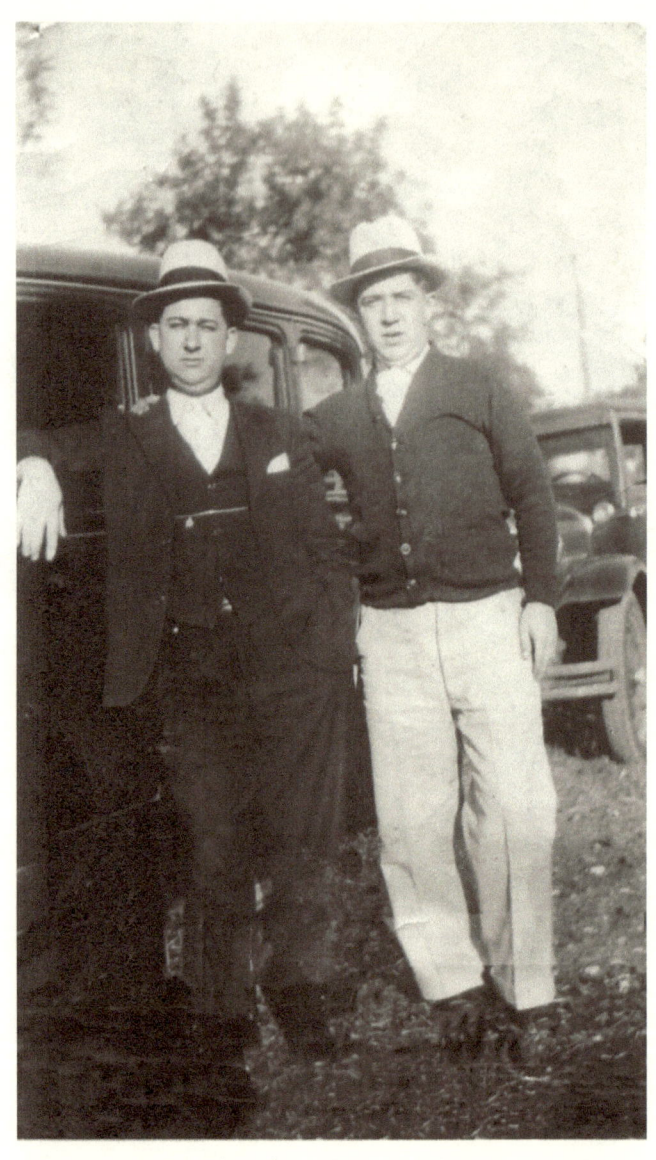

George Avgerinos (on the left) and younger brother, Dan Avgerinos.

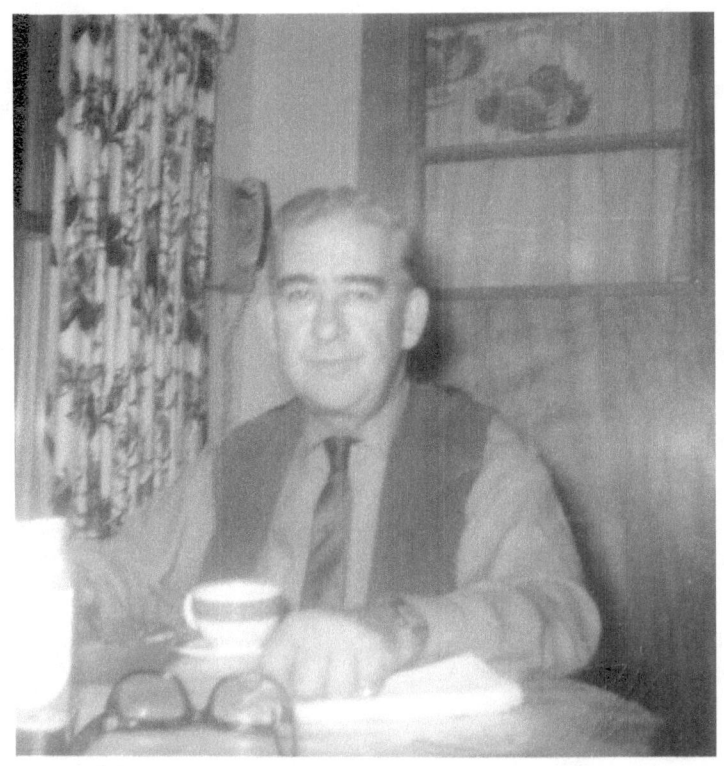

George Avgerinos, *circa* 1968.

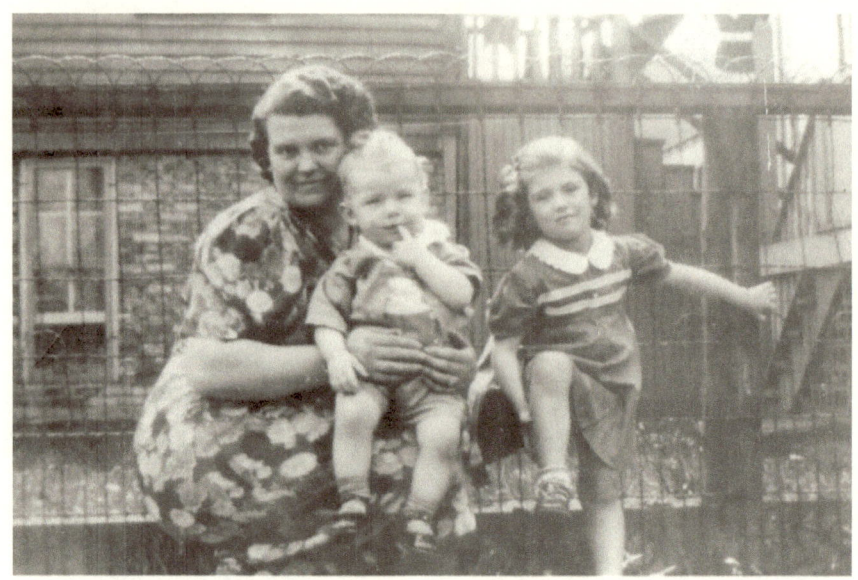

Helen Avgerinos and her two youngest children of five (from left): Dan and Gina, *circa* 1938.

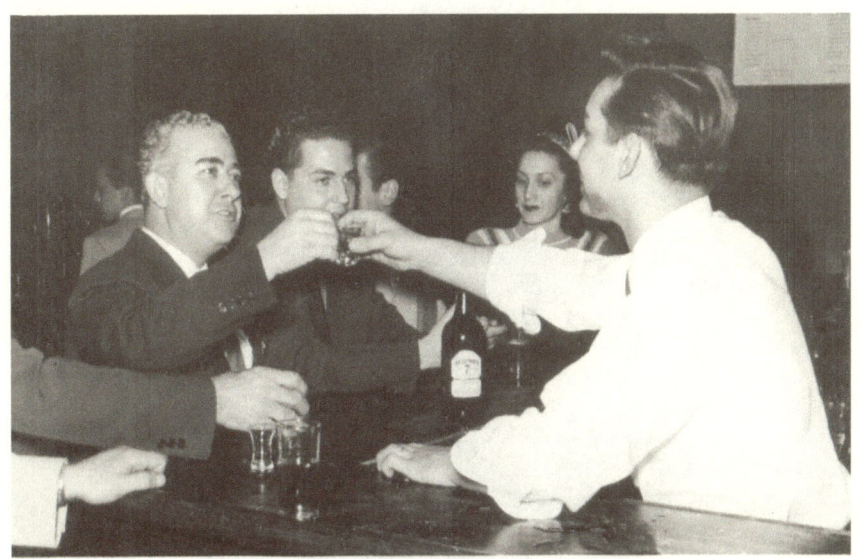

George Avgerinos (on the left) and Gus Kalamaras (George's uncle and godfather) toasting at George's older brother Perry's christening; June Avgerinos (George's aunt) is in the background (on the right), *circa* 1953.

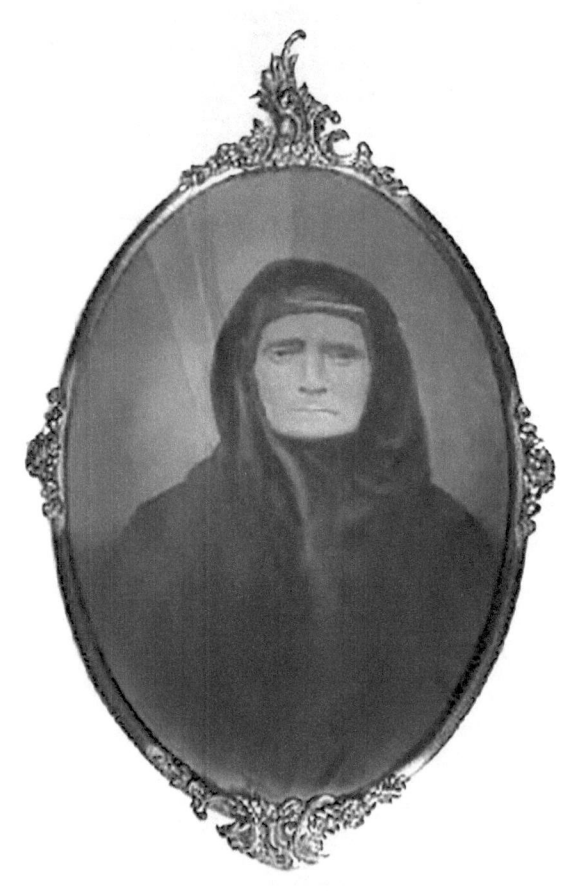

Konstantina Kalamaras (George's paternal great-grandmother).

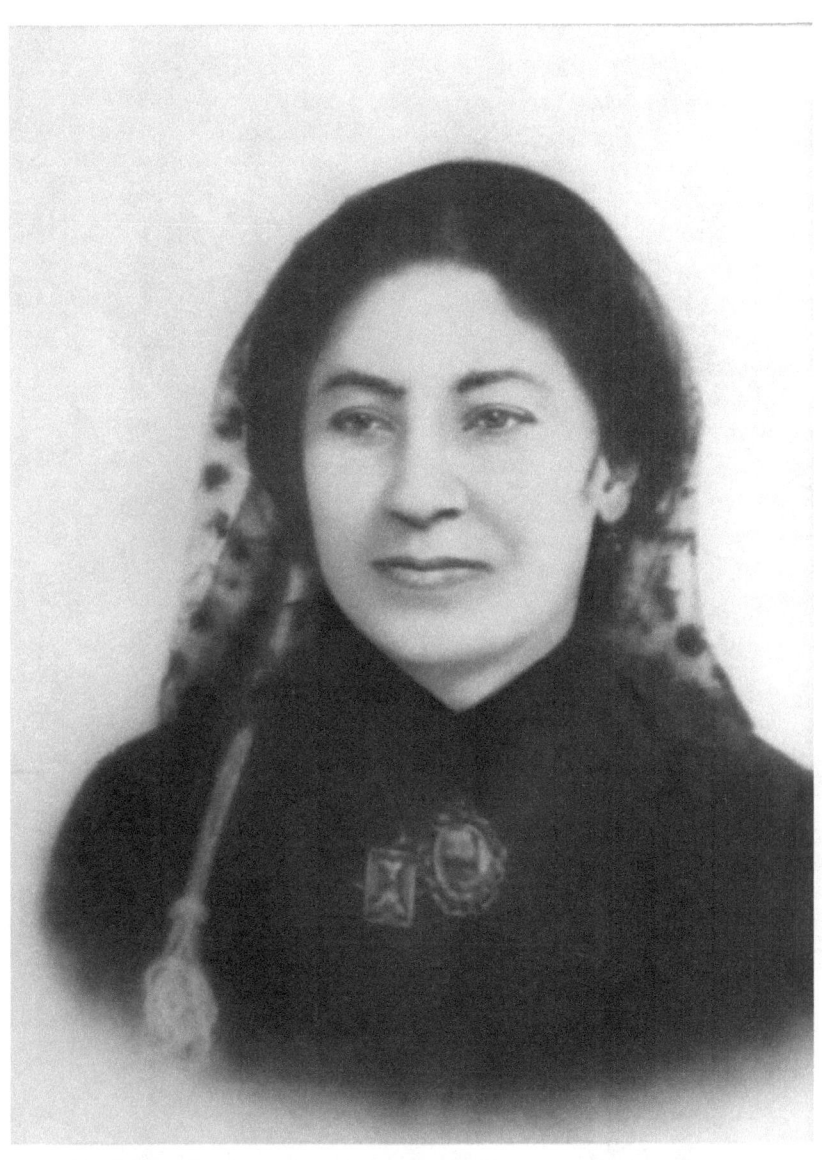

Vasiliki Demopoulos (George's paternal great-grandmother).

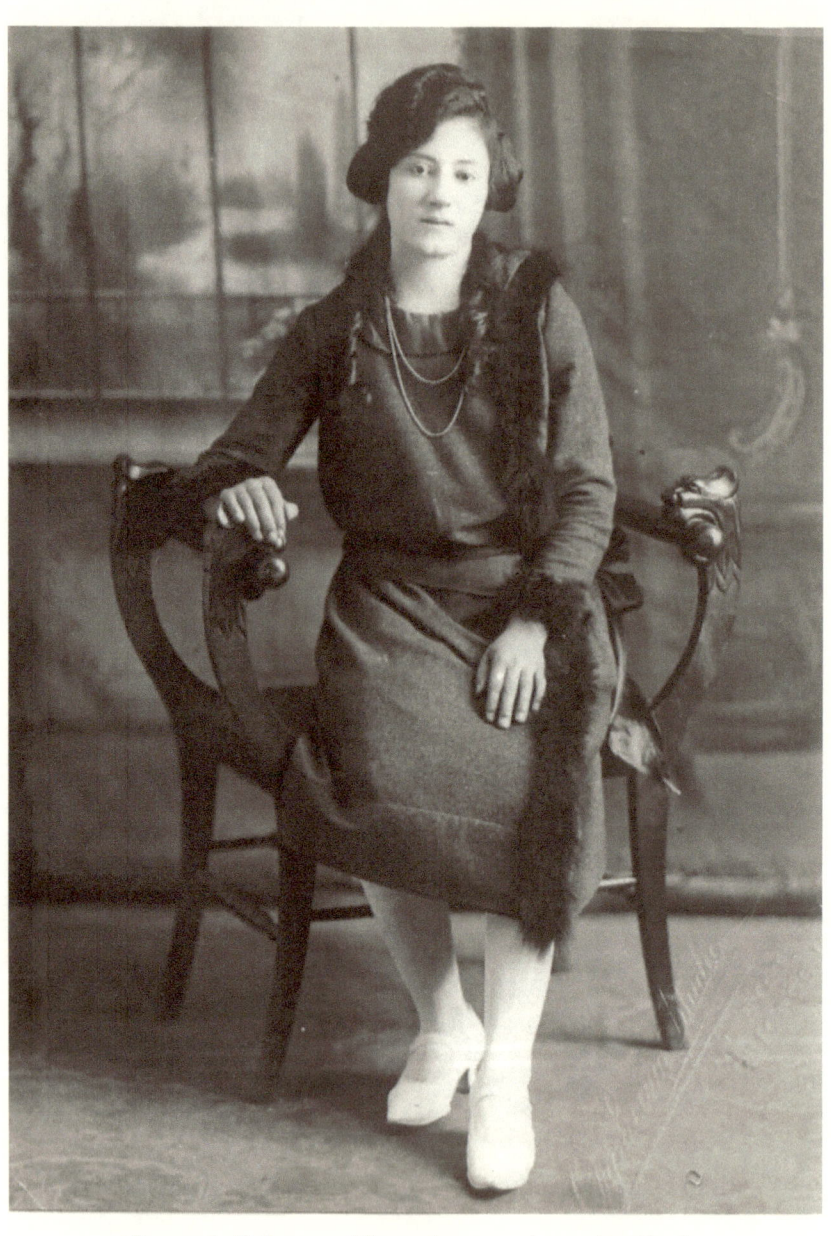

Stavroula Kalamaras (George's paternal grandmother).

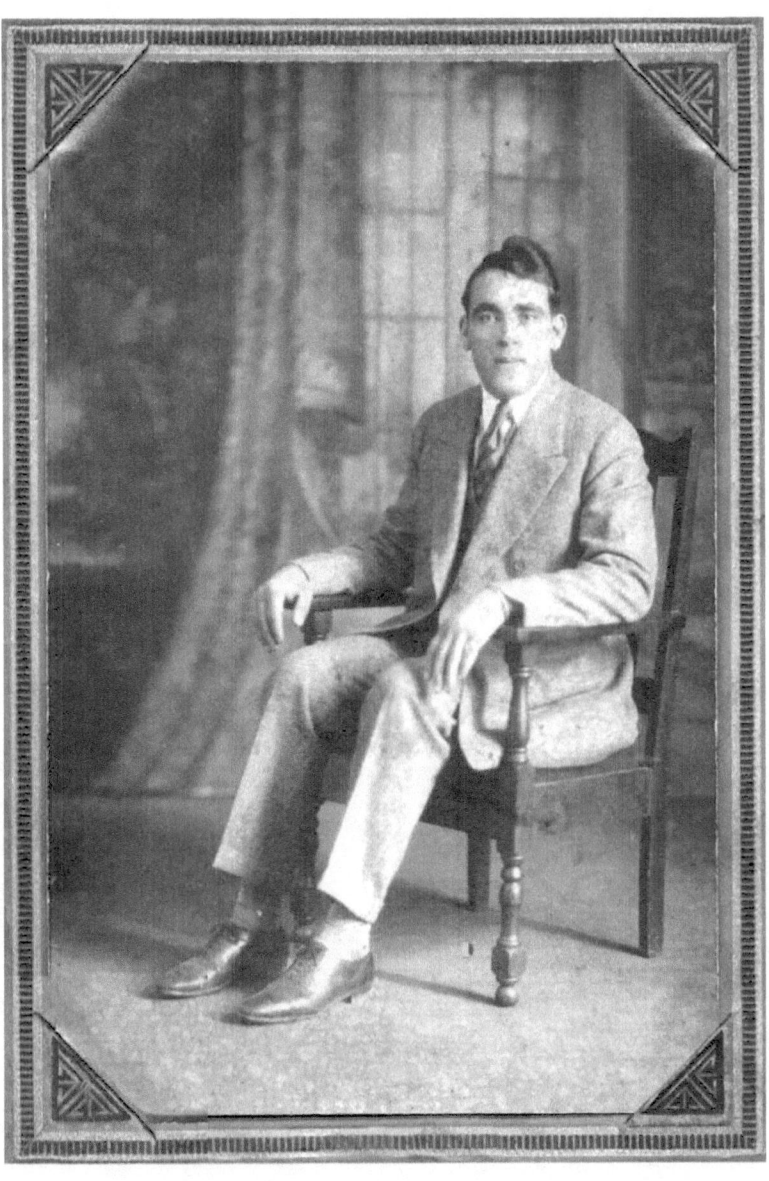

Pericles Kalamaras (George's paternal grandfather).

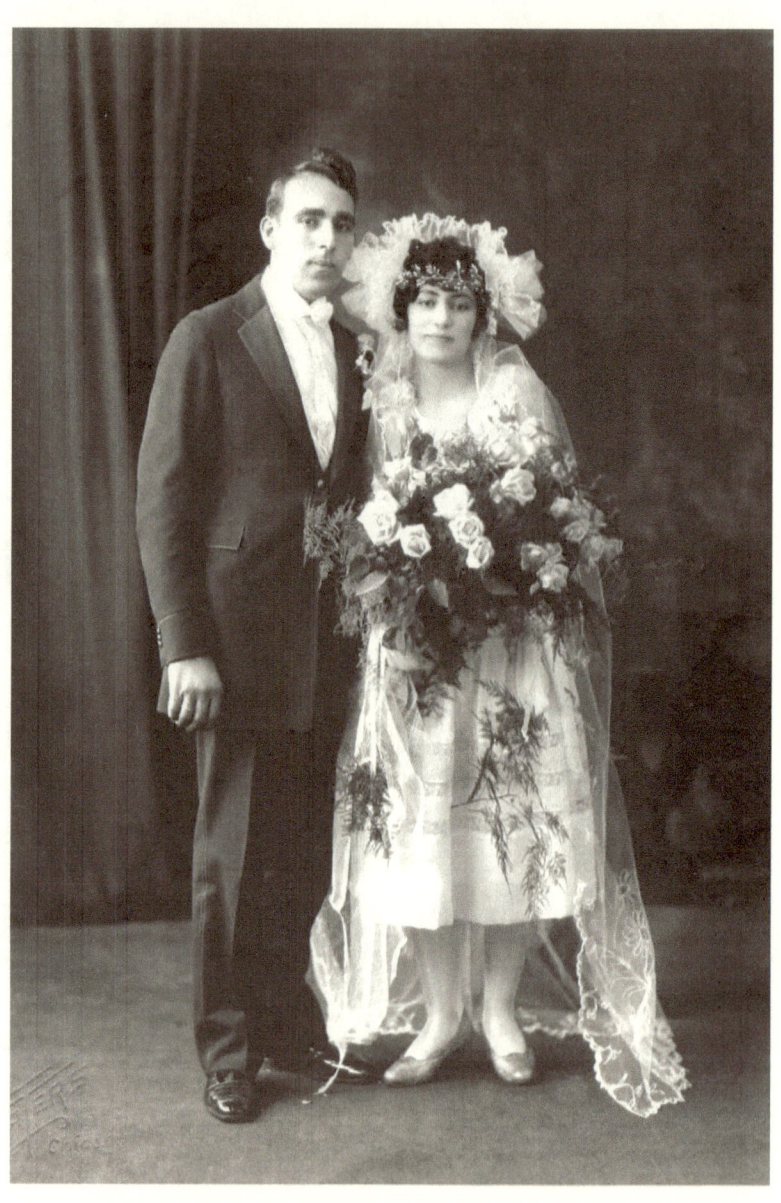

Pericles and Stavroula Kalamaras on their wedding day, 1927.

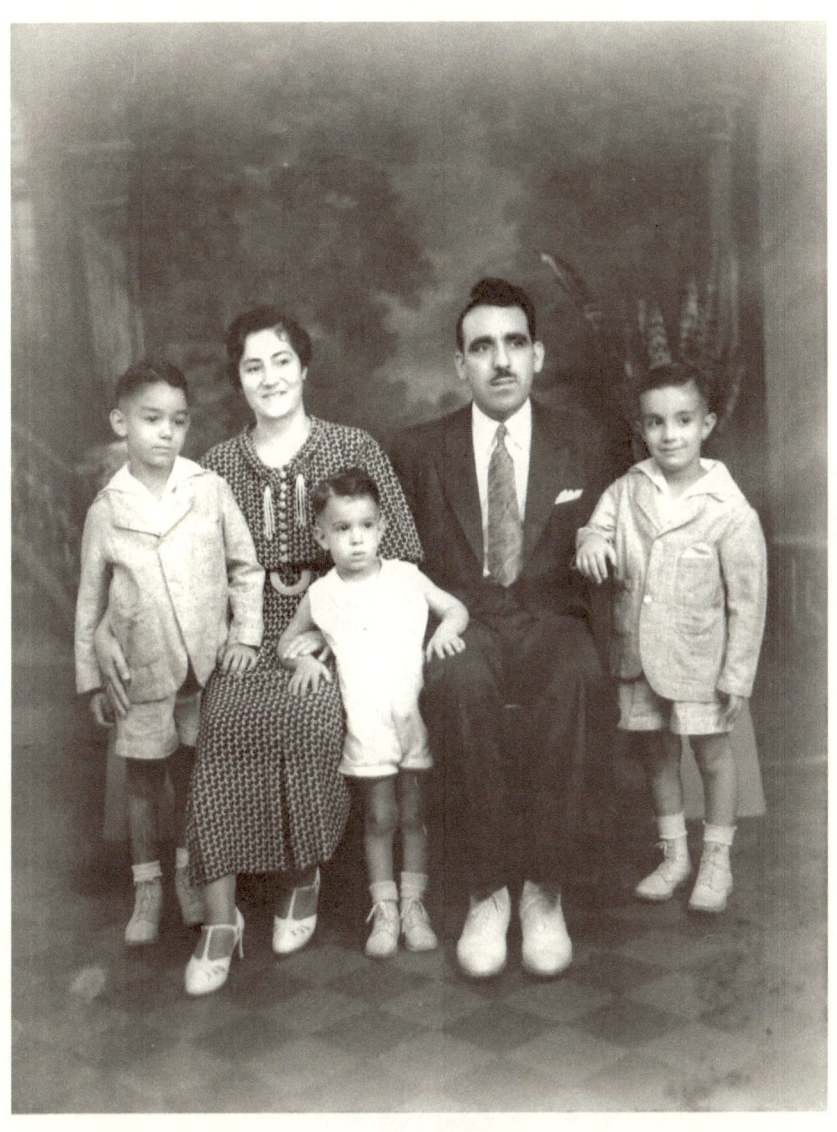

Stavroula and Pericles Kalamaras and three of their four children (from left): Gus (George's godfather), Bill (George's father), and Alex. Georgene (Dimas) was not yet born at the time of this photo, *circa* 1934.

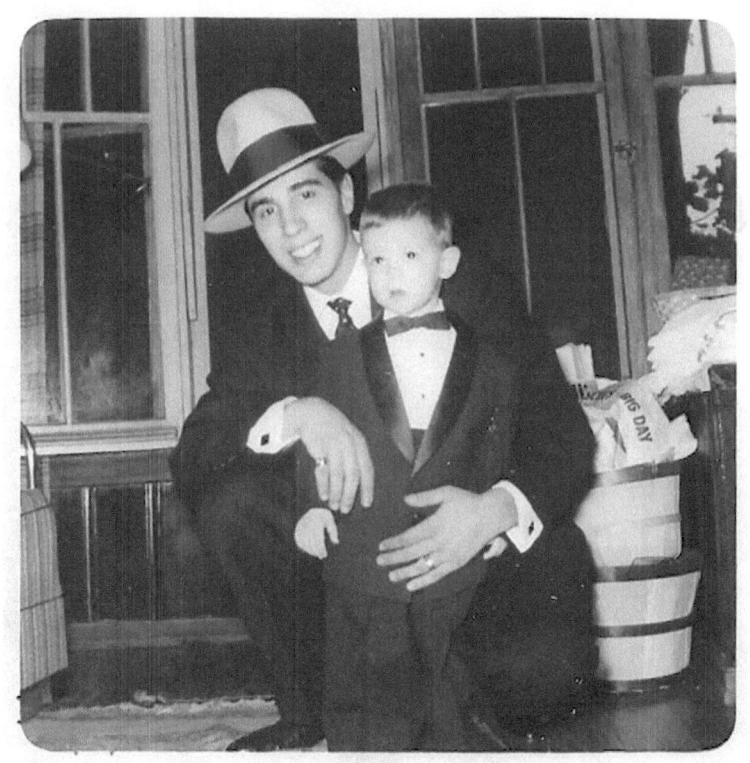

Bill (Vasilios) Kalamaras (George's father) and Perry Kalamaras
(George's brother), 1955.

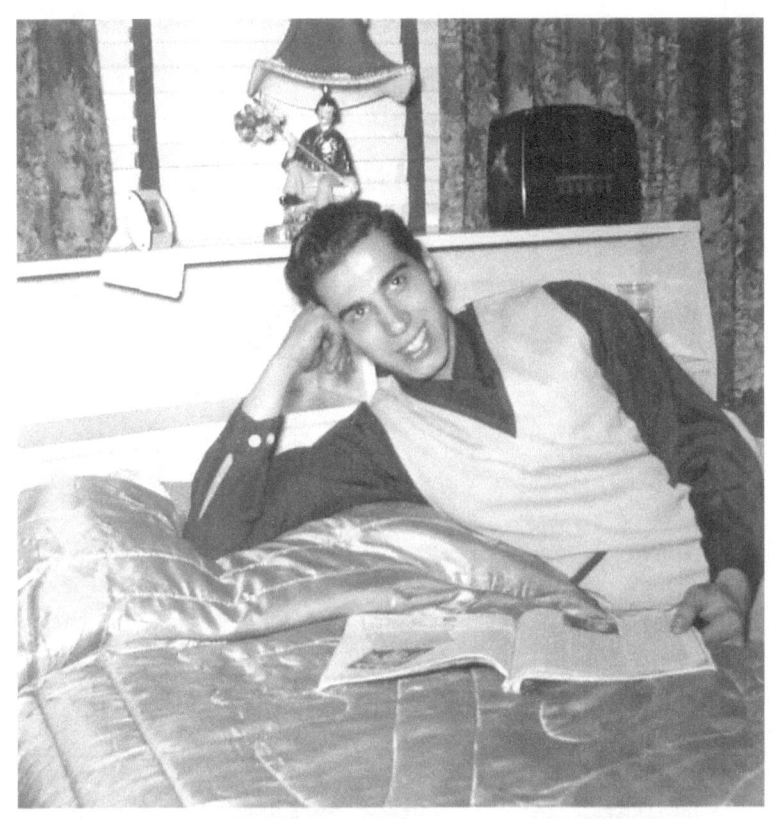

Bill Kalamaras, *circa* 1954.

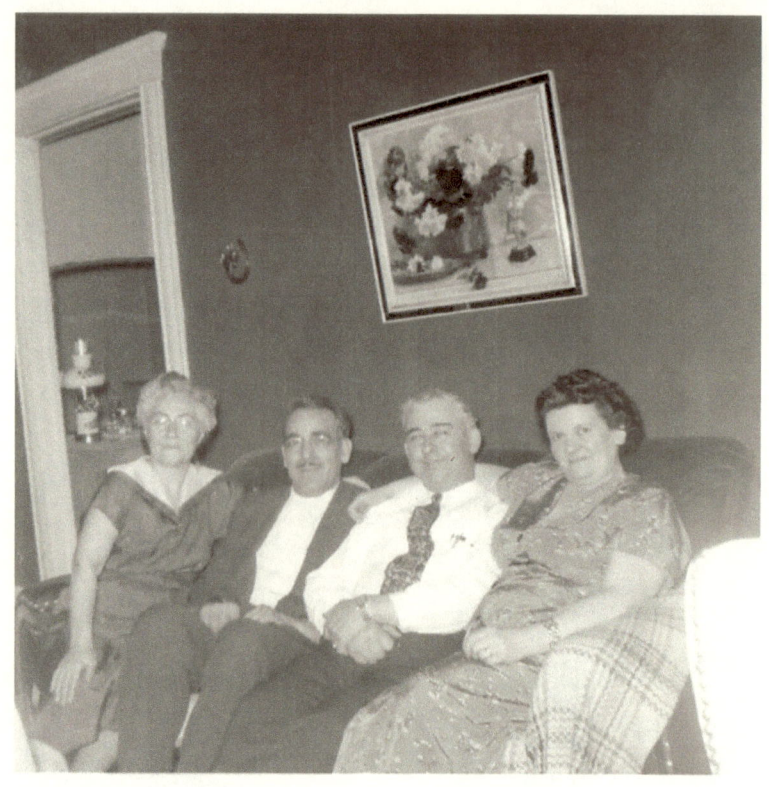

(From left): Stavroula Kalamaras, Pericles Kalamaras, George Avgerinos, and Helen Avgerinos, *circa* 1954.

The preceding photographs are courtesy of Dan Avgerinos, Georgene Dimas, and George Kalamaras, from their family archives.

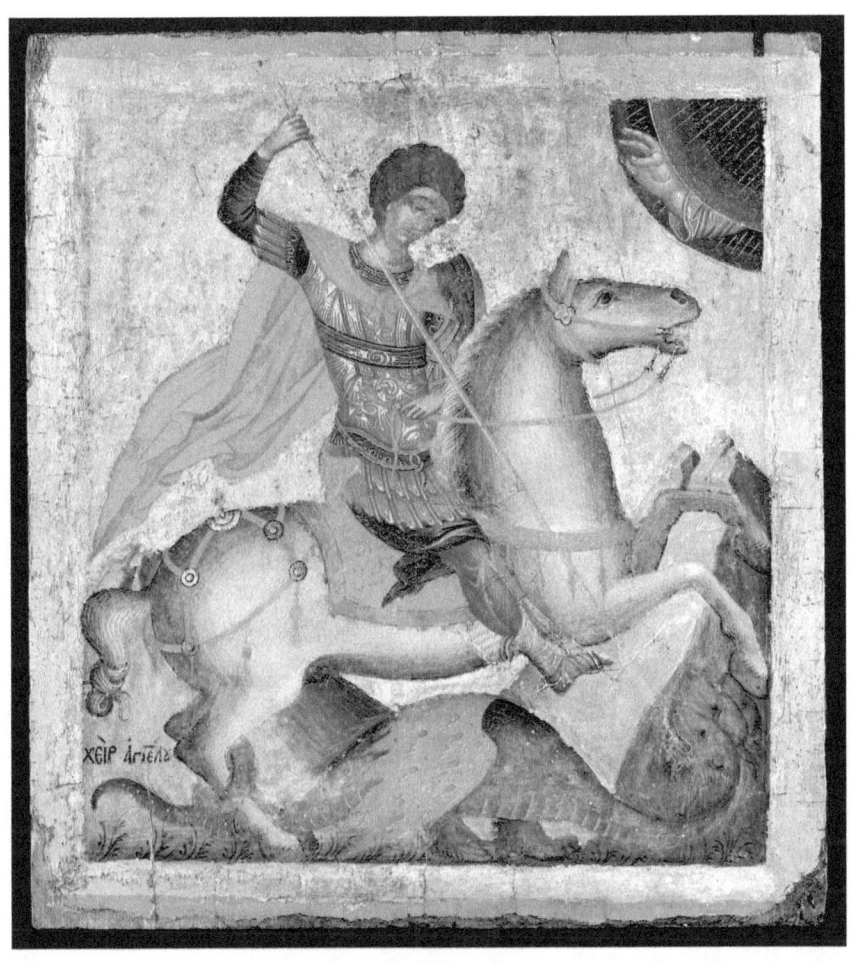

Icon of St. George.

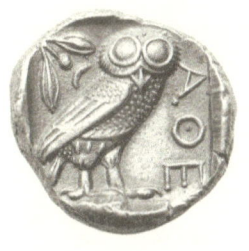

SEVEN

Tiny Movements of the Throbbing World
Waiting for Us

A Reading from the Epistle of Gisèle Prassinos

as heard by Paul Éluard at the Bureau of Surrealist Research

And so, my brothers, let your cigarette burn as if a cypress
tree in Ephesus on fire. Once, when you were young, you
were me. And you felt your woman-body glow and expand
in ways only the wind knows. Please, there is a seasonal
wind inside each fallen leaf. And what has fallen is part of
what you hope to one day redeem. Raise. Lift. Listen. There
is an eviction of geese leaving the body all at once when we
awake. And we are rarely awake. Stop. Step. Hear. Your voice
is my voice is what the deep wells of grief call up from the
ground. You lean forward in your chairs, listening to me—this
fifteen-year-old half-Greek girl who will one day become a
lantern burning water—convinced you have lost something
far back in your youth. And you have. What you have lost
is a protective scavenger. Of sound. Advice. And I am here
before you and also inside three of the two steps from the
dream bowl of blowfish left at your bedpost. I love you all
as deeply as you love yourselves. *If* you love yourselves. And
I implore you to do so. Here, in Paris. Here, in Ephesus.
Here, where the vast weight of those who are cypress-stung
swings in the in-between. My brothers of the Institute of
Scientific Exploration. My sisters of the wind lifting through
the soles of the feet. Go inward. Toward me. Toward. Yourself.
Toward every bird you know you are longing to wing-shoot
and become. Fifteen is just a beak rip. Age has no worm. Or
mouse. Or drift of vowel. This is true and not true. And it has
been so for as long as we have lied to one another with our
various truths. Listen to these words. Even as you eat them,
they disappear.

Lord Byron Discovers the Poetry of César Vallejo Inscribed in the Delphic Stone

He read it, they say, and then he died.

Fever took him in Missolonghi, Aetolia.

Our voices are forever inscribed in the ether, he had mused.

We might step forward from the wake of our words.

When César Vallejo died, Lord Byron died a second time.

Let's set sail on a boat strong and proud as the *Hercules*.

It is said that it is good *not* to die at home. Like Vallejo in Paris.

And Lord Byron in Peru.

And the Aztecs in Greece on the plains of Thermopylae.

And George Seferis in Fort Wayne, Indiana.

Now we descend into the Delphic depths.

We encounter words there, the omphalos of the world.

Words wait for us. Inscribe us.

Throughout all time, time languidly lulls.

It was Byron who said,

Ζώη μου, σας αγαπώ (*Zoë mou, sas agapo*)—

And we hear it from the depths.

We hear it in the tender antennae of an ant.

Tiny movements of the throbbing world waiting for us.

Ζώη μου, σας αγαπώ (*Zoë mou, sas agapo*)—

My life, César Vallejo. Your words in stone. My life, I love you.

Cavafy's Craving

Cavafy claimed he had become
        quite deaf. Something like a spur
               below the tongue when he read

the indentations of snow
        in a cypress tree. Wind-blur in his belly,
               in leaves moiling from the corpse's mouth,

inside each cave-drawn burr illuminated
        on goatskin in the *History of Nicephorus*
               Gregoras. And as for the oil lamp he carried

from room to room those nights
        he roamed for doves. And as for the tongue
               of a lover he longed to lull toward both

of their dissolve. And for Constantinople
        constantly conspiring against his memory
               of Athens, even against the shyness

of the lamp, as he glimpsed a crescent-shaped scar
        on his Aunt Cora's thigh exposed one evening
               moment, as she bent to scrub the stone

floor in untucked moonlight. Trust.
        Not virtue. Lust. In the lack
               and length of his paper and pen,

and in all the ecstatic eel cravings
        like hot wax embedded in his tongue.
                In his ears. Saddle soap of swaying

ossicles. Stirrups. Inside his tormented
        fasts. And what a moth he held so
                thrumming shut against the closed fist

of the world. Deaf. Velvet. Sting
        beat of anemic green with one dark eye
                widening inside each wing. A thistle.

A cocklebur below the tongue. His tongue, dead
        tongue. Alive with the ancestry of a cypress
                root in snow. In Athens. Cavafy's craving.

Sung backward as a smalling
        toward song. Quite deaf. Quite
                breath. Quite ear hair curving his advancing

years far back from the stirrup and the urge.
        For love of stinging the world,
                Constantine Cavafy craved and wept

and—he claimed—even went deaf.
        And splayed his most private tongue,
                split with spit, slung with dove-blood.

Constant as Constantinople. Censer sway
        of liturgical leaves. Nile clouds clotting the smoke-
                taste trace. An unrequited tongue, or coming

untucked as Aunt *this* or Uncle *that*.
       As the endless debate over the sensual
             merits of Athens or Alexandria.

And the chance by lamplight at his writing
       table each night to chart a past. The chance
             to camphor from room to room an oil

in the cave of his left ear, an accident
       of moths momentarily exposed
             far from the anemic-green

light of Athens. To stay alive. Another
       night. Constantly. In his absence.
             To finally live a life. To lie.

Twelve Reasons Why Ritsos Wrote *Scripture of the Blind* Only for Those Who See

1. In the dark, it's easier to see the number one once than to see the number two twice.

2. Let's say the inept Colonels of the 1960s were quite similar to the Metaxas Generals of the 30s, except with fewer medals and shoulder patches. Let's say every freedom lover named their first born boy *Lefteris*—short for *Eleftherios* (meaning *free, the liberator* or *bite this apple with your termite ear or with the left ventricle of your heart*).

3. Because when we look in the mirror with only one of our eyes, what stares back is the other eye, somehow floating there, disembodied, broken.

4. *If you read the lost Gospel of Judas Iscariot you understand what a non-precious metal silver really is*, Ritsos said to no one in particular.

5. During a military coup, and in the afterbath of rain, we might beg lightning to cache itself comfortably in our mouths.

6. *Blind Man's Bluff is more a game of deception than bonding*, Lefteris thought. *The population in Council Bluffs, Iowa, is even less than that in Scottsbluff, Nebraska—though slightly more than that in Bluffton, Indiana.*

7. Let's say the Gospel of Mary Magdalene (even with its ten missing pages) was the one most read during Sunday

mornings at five—the time of both the resurrection and of the house arrest of all the red biting fire ants, which seem to espouse communism as they collectively carry away a twig from a termite mound fortified within a statue of Athena.

8. Because when George Seferis looks in the mirror, first he sees the smoldering coals of his pipe. Then comes the splintered moon from his birthplace near Smyrna, the moon aching through the bones of Odysseus Elytis, whom Seferis is certain is hiding, there, behind him, in the knots in the knotty pine walls of his study.

9. We might call yesterday, *yesterday*. But only if we begin doing so three and one-third days after tomorrow.

10. Counting each of Jesus' twelve very capable disciples, we wonder what prevented anointing Lazarus as a thirteenth—to follow the Christ, even write a Gospel once he relinquished the stench of his previously dead mouth. Was Lazarus busy writing his own *Scripture of the No-Longer Dead*?

11. *I honestly don't know. I don't know why they shot me,* Lefteris winced, leaning across the Athens bar. *And now I can't tell if I'm living or just slightly more alive.*

12. *In the dark, it's much harder to count to thirteen than to twelve,* Ritsos proclaimed, as if in reply. As if a zodiac of words. As if a zodiac revealed itself, there, in star charts in the slope of a bee intestine dissected by a recalcitrant astronomer.

13. Look at the night sky through the aroused navel of your Belovèd. Count—there—each of your fingers and toes. It all adds up to an angry weather pattern we might leave as luck in a trashcan waiting at the curbside to be nominated as the only sane member of the Divine Trust of *The Sound and Sacred Word*. Epaulets, say, disguised as a vague mustache. The scriptural equivalent of the blind little brother of *The Sacred and the Profane*.

How the World Keeps Dying Through Dinos Christianopoulos

> *what didn't you do to bury me*
> *but you forgot that I was a seed*
> —Dinos Christianopoulos

Too bad the world kept dying
inside him. There was an icon

of a beheaded saint. Starlings
fiercing it out in his brain. Even the sad

hand of a concerto for winds
and timpani by Petros Petridis.

There was flitching and corpse candles
and ghost smoke and stout-willed

sorrow. Thus, Dinos Christianopoulos
considered the small crimes of human skin,

of casson the cattle and goats left him with.
Such stories of sorrow lodged in the rafters of his den.

In the amber lamps. Yes, he hung just two
photos on his walls: those of the poet Constantine Cavafy

and Vassilis Tsitsanis, the great *rembetika* and *laiko* singer.
Sure, he remained Orthodox despite his nightly meanderings

through the chest cavities of dead crows confining
the light. He remembered how the rain ached

through him, even in sun. How the sun burned
a blister of moon cankering the snow in his throat.

How he needed the study of dentistry
to understand the shavings of his bowels.

The reading of tea leaves to annunciate
stars. The color of his donkey's gums

to determine the time of day. Call him
gay, and the trapdoor blows apart

its dynamite hinge. Call him Cavafy's clone,
and the glue of the book binding becomes

his mouth. The world keeps
living, keeps dying, keeps trying

to entomb him for good. *Plato*, he announced. *Aristotle*,
he shivered into the wind. *Socrates. Pythagoras.*

Even Protagoras, he screamed. Stars slunk down
through him into cruel caves of almost-crystalline sleep.

Look at the chewing gum beneath my shoe, he said as if
biting back the wind. *Even Van Gogh decided he was done*

listening to the sorrow of the world and all it tries
to bury in its greed. In what it believes is a seedless plea.

The Life of Nicolas Calas

1907   Born Nikos Kalamaris in Lausanne, Switzerland, on a
       starless night beneath a cypress where two owls were
       mating. Calas grows up in Athens. His father was
       said to have perfected the little-known sport of "wind-
       spitting." His mother, Rosa Caradja, was the great-
       granddaughter of Markos Botsaris, military leader and
       hero of the Greek War of Independence.

1913   Takes first piano lessons but learns, as his teacher
       described, "how to replicate the sound of wind in
       the throat of a sparrow." His teacher vows to expand
       Calas's knowledge "so that he can also play the sound
       of mud drinking mud."

1922   Rebels against his wealthy family background and
       becomes a Trotskyite, in light of the 1922 Asia
       Minor catastrophe and refugees pouring into Athens.
       Calas, whose birth name is "Kalamaris" (derived
       from "squid"), begins a series of recurring dreams
       in which he writes poems, but they disappear "into
       the coral reefs of the brain." Calas begins studying
       psychoanalytic theory to try to decipher the slow
       motion of underwater lamps that call to him nightly
       in his dreams.

1925- Studies Law and Political Science at the University of
1930   Athens. Active in the radical Student Society. Begins
       reading Breton, Soupault, and Desnos in French.
       Starts writing poetry regularly and begins ritual
       of burying half-finished poems in the gardens of

strangers. Develops a fondness for eating fried worms and vows to never again pray to the moon.

1932   Calas's debut, *Poems* (Ποιήματα), is published. One of the first true modernists in Greece, Calas is clearly ahead of his time and suffers some negative criticism. He experiences "voices of anger" from his bed clothes, which, as he describes, refuse to warm him through the cooler Athens nights. He begins wondering whether he should take back his birth name, Kalamaris, believing it might grant him ocean courage against negative literary voices. Then he dismisses that thought and begins a period of divination with the bones of mice. Only then does he seek out an explanation from his father about the specifics of "wind-spitting."

1934-   Calas becomes a member of Breton's Surrealist circle
1937   in Paris. The 1936 coup of General Metaxas forces him to leave Greece permanently. While in Paris, he befriends Yvette George, a dancehall performer rumored to be the illegitimate daughter of Gérard de Nerval. Smitten by George, Robert Desnos falls madly in love with her. And Calas, though only seeking friendship with George, begins having a series of waking dreams in which they walk hand in hand across town together—always at the exact moment Desnos performs his "sleep sessions." Calas begins collecting discarded lobster claws, hiding them beneath his pillow so as to "conjure dreams of Yvette's most honorable father," as he confides to a few friends.

1939   Leaves France at the onset of the Second World War.
        Arrives in Lisbon. Forced to stay there into 1940,
        at which time he forges a visa, with mysteriously
        precise instructions given him by a secret message slid
        beneath his hotel door. He hears the sounds of birds
        everywhere, particularly in violin music from street
        musicians. He becomes convinced he can fly, though
        never tests his conviction, but instead begins deep
        conversations with street food vendors as a way "to
        ground" himself.

1940   Leaves for the United States and settles in New York,
        establishing a Surrealist group. Learns to "crochet my
        voice," as he proclaims, though the theory of *Surrealist
        Crochetism* that he advocates is never quite understood
        and fails to take root.

1943-   Marries the divorcée Elena von Hoershelman in 1943,
1952   a Russian-born psychoanalyst with whom he would
        go on to collaborate on a number of research projects,
        articles, and books. Calas becomes a research
        associate and consultant for the renowned
        anthropologist Margaret Mead. In 1953, their
        collaboration results in the publication of an
        anthropological anthology entitled *Primitive Heritage*,
        which Calas swears is actually a cache of food and not
        a book.

1956   Has a series of recurring "squid" dreams, which had
        subsided for three decades. While in New York,
        through a dream, he learns of the birth of someone

named George Kalamaras in Chicago. Calas, whose own birth name is "Kalamaris," becomes obsessed with the dream as the name of the Chicago Greek is similar to his but differs slightly in spelling. He researches the theory of "proactive dreaming" and renews contact with Gaston Bachelard in Paris, attempting to uncover the metaphorical dimensions of his dreams, which—he is convinced—have been instigated by the rustling of owls outside his bedroom window. It is during this period that Bachelard prescribes Zen koans to help Calas uncover the mysteries of his various periods of dreaming; he additionally suggests that this Chicago Kalamaras (even if just a figment of fancy) may one day also become a Greek Surrealist poet. Calas scoffs at the idea, but his dreams of the Chicago Kalamaras cease.

1960s Calas pursues a career as an art critic and as a lecturer of art history at Farleigh Dickinson University. It is during this time that he develops an interest in Emily Dickinson and Charles Dickens. Like many of his previous interests, this develops into an obsession. His psychoanalytic therapist, Henri Mashon, prescribes that Calas write letters to himself and abandon poetry. Instead, Calas writes poems, mailing them to himself, but soon develops an obsession with stamp collecting as a result of receiving so many envelopes addressed in a hand he cannot quite recognize.

1970s Calas attempts to contact Desnos to renew "joint dreaming," forgetting that Desnos left the body at the close of the Second World War.

1988   Dies in New York, his wife, Elena, at his
side. He asks for a pen on his deathbed and
(recalling his koan work decades earlier with
Bachelard) attempts to write a Japanese Zen
master death poem. He begins "I," vehemently
shakes his head "no," and then releases his final
breath. Elena verifies that as he wrote (and
simultaneously spoke) "I," an owl perched on
the windowsill near his deathbed, leaving a freshly
killed mouse before flying away. Calas's *Complete
Poems*—all in the manner of Surrealism—is
published posthumously, with an unsigned preface
written by an unknown poet.

Maria Efstathiadi Confronts Time in the Bending of Rain

The transgressions
The transgressions, you thought
Which start in the legs
The fire-driven thighs
The inattentive brain
The transgressive act of loving
Simple things like rain
Like coffee, say, or tea, clocks that have stopped
Sentences without end, without the words, *word* or *thing*
Dreams with no names
Naming us when sleep sleeps
Naming you naming me
With their fog
With their thick animal mist
You and the holy ones, Maria
The dead see things
We don't
Care to even want to know
The dead are thriving inside
The living
Partitions of our mouths
Words our words work and want
To break apart each time a moment is ignored
Each time the tongue gives up
On us and tries to wag loose
All it tries to say
In the driving rains
That hammer at and lament and bend us
Like broken clocks
Whose hands, contorted, have given up on them
Entirely, giving in, to the stiffening drift of rain

Soma: It Is Raining, Stratis Haviaras

Waves of tortoise hair pour down, the way women's voices enter us as they touch each other open in separate rooms.

*

Mist lifts from the long rain of a rock the corpse exhales into its fragrant grass sprouting near his chest. Above which a bee-eater and jackdaw linger.

*

What we move toward in the long grass is what we once were held by. Root of moonlight. Centipede in dusk.

*

The sky storms down like the insomniac's color he descends toward through the burning stairwell in his cigarette.

*

The dark wood of the knife respects the slice of onion, alone on its wooden board. *It is not easy*, the knife thinks, *being an onion*.

*

An onion of sleep drifts near the scent of lovers, alone in separate cities, lying still in blossoming milk their soil leaves.

*

What a man sees through a woman's dream darkens what he hears through.

*

A young girl roams pothole to pothole in the war-blistered streets. Her voice opens, like something final, a huge hope in a drop of milk.

Kostis Palamas Does Not Attend His Own Funeral

The whole of Greece rests in this coffin.
—Angelos Sikelianos

One day, the wind leaves the body. For good.

If we're lucky, it releases. Clings to the leaves. To the silver veins of the olives.

Then the next day it is February 28, 1943. Forever. Sometimes for good, sometimes not. Thus, 100,000 Greeks come out for the funeral. For Kostis Palamas's funeral. Ignoring mandates of the German Occupation. Angelos Sikelianos reciting his poem "Palamas" at the service, reminding the world that, *The whole of Greece rests in this coffin.*

Then the wind shifts. The leaves shift. The earth seems to almost weep its night dew back into the air. Takis Sinopoulos scuffs his feet and cries out. Miltos Sahtouris, unable to bear it, stays in his apartment and frantically rips a toenail, then lights a cigarette he forgets to smoke. Yannis Ritsos strokes the lump in his throat, remembering a donkey he kept as a child—and his weeping when it walked the stone path with him and died.

Then Palamas is placed. In the grave. *His* grave. Though it is not Palamas. But the body of Greece. The whole of it and more. Mumps of mud and leaves. Polio of grapes and sheep. Broken bones of the sea. Restless and wrecked. Swollen from a swastika of bees.

And 100,000 Athenians sing the Greek national anthem, sounding like vowels from the owl's mouth. One man shouting, *Long live the liberty of spirit!* The crowd responding, *Long live Liberty!*—as if wind-swept in the salt of olives.

And the luck of the leaves cries out, *We are the leaves, the luck of the leaves. Leaves that shape the wind and welcome you back.*

And Kostis Palamas drifts, then sits on a hill. A hill of trees. Reciting his poems against the Occupation—certain salve of Greece that is its history and its disease.

And the wind shifts. The breath shifts. And he is gone. Then he is not gone. Kostis Palamas is everywhere at once. In the Greeks. In the Germans. In Aristotle and Sophocles. In the ships at sea. In Odysseus tied to the mast. Crying out. Straining the ropes. Hearing a song he longs to tongue and seed. As Palamas searches for the notes. For the words. And the words within those words. As he searches for his belovèd Greece. The whole of it. Resting. Moving. Caught somewhere between the old world and the new. And he is there floating. In death. And more death. In the confusion of the in-between.

Manolis Kalomiris, Leaving for the Hospital for the Last
   Time Before His Death, Places on His Desk His
   Unfinished *Symphony of the Simple and Good People*

He spoke for many years, girdled by a voluptuous
tree. His *Symphony of the Simple and Good*

People. Manolis Kalomiris
sometimes was a steppe eagle

clarifying the poplars. There was a Mother
of Charity in his chest. St. Sofia sat inside him

sipping tea. To eat lamb stew between each oboe
solo allowed him enough strength to stand

against all the boils of the war years. The moon
beckoned his throat where cricket scratch lanced

notes he then transcribed into frankincense
and depth. If you asked him why music

resembled a bicycle on the wrong side
of the street, he'd tell you to cut out your tongue

and examine it through the wrong end
of a telescope. Then listen to the silence

your moaning attempts to crack. Wind congealed
in his throat like fluid scuffed from broken bones

he was born into searching for sunspots
of love. Born through the pelvic bones

of a cypress root, Manolis Kalomiris
heard his name repeated many times

in the salt beards of the many-soaked.
As if he was searching the underworld

for what was above. As if
he was Odysseus lamenting

a home he never had
but only discovered when he wept there.

Nanos Valaoritis Visits Paul Bowles in Morocco

And they smoke hash together in Tangier and pass
the hookah and, yes, it is dark. The night soil
they burn for fuel gives off the scent of earth
turning and turned. And the thick animal night
inside the wind is inside their bodies
as well. Wind from his heart, Valaoritis's heart,
merging with the leaves of a Paul Bowles tree,
desert-stretched and sunk. Roots reaching
for water all the way to the sea. Nanos reads
his latest poems to Bowles. *Into* Bowles.
They are not words or sounds or aches of rain.
They are splices of wind, spittle, bits of ash from his rib.
His sixth and seventh ribs on his left side,
Nanos Valaoritis's side, perched there like crows
counting corn growth on an abacus.

Bowles passes him, again, the hookah, praising
what they share, some of which is exile—from the public,
from the junta, from *The Sheltering Sky*. Bowles asks
about Breton and Péret and whether it's true
that René Daumal actually died in India with a peacock
sewn slantwise into his chest. *Love the life*
with which the wind gifts you, Valaoritis answers. *Look*
in the mirror after painting it black as sea salt
sunk in a bog. That, Paul, is Surrealism.

And the wind in their bones, in *both* of their bones,
lifts a little and burns like birdsong through the hollow
parts of the heart. Men and women emerge as outlines

from dreams with canisters of wren feathers
they add to the hookah, along with snail droppings
and bits of chickweed.

There are imprints in the ether, forms in the shape
every word ever lost. Forms in the shape
of Simone Kahn, Jacqueline Lamba, a sandhill crane
from Ogallala, Nebraska, with one leg poised into a pout
of mud as it scours for fish. This could be a wood ibis
or a marabou stork, the scent of a sewing machine
on a dissecting table, even the effects of the hash. Valaoritis
hands Paul Bowles his beret, asking if that shade
of black is dark enough to spark the mirror
he spoke of minutes before, Bowles handing back
his hooded Moroccan wool cloak as one way to be
a wingèd birdman and fly above it all.

And they wash their hands and step from their room
and clear their throats of the smoke, approaching
the casbah in search of tagine chicken and a bit
of mint tea. And each person they pass is a poem
Bowles and Valaoritis read and seem to know
and pour into one another. The night soil
keeps burning the city streets and the dreams
embedded in their lungs. And the thick animal night
offers healing release, beckoning down into them
as they hunch near the tagine oven and praise the chicken
they are about to eat. Say its wings,
even dead, are as moving as the poems of Elytis,
Sahtouris, and Breton. The gift they are certain
is sure to enter them and lift their urge
beyond the burden of words and into the driftings
of daylight and the release of all discernible disease.

Alexander Contemplates a Map
of the Then-Known World

It seemed so small even in its largeness
Alexander went to the stables
To pat his great horse Bucephalus
The animal he tamed and that was also large
What lay ahead he did not know
Except that the world might be known
And the air in his lungs might move forward
Beyond Macedonia
Beyond Greece
Into new sands and trees
How might the plant life and the animals receive him?
What would they think of all the killing that lay beyond
The blood the phalanxes the multiple wounds?
His teacher Aristotle taught him to consider
The life inside every rock every tree each bee-sting breeze
And yet he was about to destroy whole cities
Execute civilizations and tribes
His sleep was no help
It presented to him the grandeur and disturbance of death
And when he woke each morning he felt a bit of blood
In his lungs as if something lodged there
Was trying to pull away and work itself loose
It seemed such a small thing to feel yet it remained
Like moonlight clotting on his brow
Or on the great flanks of his horse
Whinnying a great cloud of breath illuminated by the moon
The world was to be conquered he thought
Known even in its unknowing
Even in the darkness that threatened to cull the moon
Its canyons trenches and worms and sink
It into the refreshing death of its shadowy miraculous seas

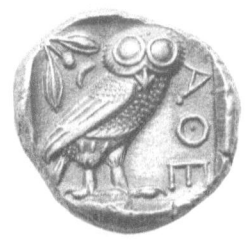

EIGHT

For My Family

The Death(s) of Pericles Kalamaras

1834–1895 & 1895–1961

1.

How strange, great-grandfather, to be kicked
by a horse in Pharaklatha and killed. Suddenly,
your son inherited your name, something rarely
passed father to son by Greeks. So at thirty days old,
my grandfather *also* became Pericles
in remembrance of your life and the horse
that took it.

       What were you thinking at that moment
of impact? Did you have time to consider
your wife, Konstantina? Your six sons?
Where, exactly, did the horse kick you?
Head? Heart? In the back
where it crushed a kidney? Where all the water
that had carried you suddenly went out?

Such details are age and dust, far back
in the Old Country, still clinging
to the underbelly of an insect
on the underside of an oregano leaf
or a sprig of basil. St. Basil himself
cared for the poor but could not
protect you from the sudden thrust
of fear the horse must have felt as you bridled it,
perhaps turning it from the sun toward
the spooky branches of its own blowing
shadow.

Did you make the sign of the cross
when the horse reared? Or did it kick you blindly
with a hind leg, standing stiffly in the stall,
ear pricked and twitched, certain you
were one of the rats it heard
the night before burrowing the hay?
Either way, I have measured the weight
many midnights, alone, of your death-groan.
It spilled out of you among horse droppings
and the persistent buzzing of flies.
And I wondered whether that breath released
brought you closer to the darkness
you knew had been waiting to reclaim you
all along.

      St. Basil also knew that darkness.
Together with Pachomius, a Desert Father,
he gave guidelines for communal monasticism
as a way to hang a lamp where prayers
fail. Where possibility ceases to be.
Even Pericles, acclaimed by the great
historian Thucydides as *the first citizen of Athens*,
succumbed to the Athens Plague, gasping
on his cot, realizing as far back as 429 B.C.E.
that moss beards the trees, and darkness
comes for kings and great citizens too.

2.

What did your son feel, great-grandfather,
all those years, knowing that only because
of an accident he carried the kingliness

of your first name? Did he wonder whether
he'd be taken suddenly too, through a spooky
sound that may have caused your horse's thrust?
Or did he think he was free of it when he crossed
the Atlantic and spoke the vowels of his name, slowly,
into the awkward ears and pronunciations of Ellis Island?

Did he think of you that afternoon
when I was only five? Driving his sister-in-law
Paraskevi to the family gathering. His heart giving out
without warning, within seconds of the stitch
in his chest? Foot sliding off the brake pedal
at a stoplight at 63rd and Ashland,
moving his death grip on the steering wheel
out into the comings and goings
of an otherwise normal Saturday?

What are we given in any final moment
when we give ourselves up, even as we try
to hang on? When we pet a horse in the morning, thinking
the day will unfold with a bit of bread and coffee, a late lunch,
and—if we're lucky—a little love, but find ourselves
instead crossing over from stop to go, from go
to everywhere at once?

Great-grandfather Pericles. And dear grandfather
Pericles. How strange for one of you to die at age sixty-one,
the other in 1961, having had your name passed between you,
as it passed among the stones and *into* them.
Like shadows flailing out into the wind's disease.
Broken bones and splintered stones. A horse
unthinkingly guiding your lives

when it suddenly spooked. What it eats,
what we *all* eat, passing the stars between us—and through.

All the waste and wanting of the world.

On the Deaths of My Great-Uncles Ioannis
and Theodorosios Demopoulos (1918 and 1919,
Respectively)

1.
There are many ways to be human. Many
ways to be born. Pieces of bread
to be picked up from the kitchen floor
and kissed. Quickly. Piles of salt to spill

as a charm into doorways. We might open
an umbrella by accident inside the house,
and a wind might lathe Laconia. Ioannis
Demopoulos suddenly dying from peritonitis

somewhere in Messenia only forty days
after encamping as a soldier. Someone
might cross their legs at a funeral in Solaki,
and Ioannis's older brother, Theodorosios,

might die a year later from the flu,
having just arrived in Chicago. Yes,
there are many ways to be human. Many
birds of wisdom, birds of prey circling

overhead. Waiting. Dogs without homes.
Cats who come up to strangers and stretch
their lives into them, gently yowling
for a kind hand. For a cup of milk.

2.

> If I could, dear Ioannis, belovèd Theodorosios,
> I'd lay you across my lap and grant you both a bath
> of hands, allowing you to sip milk from a bowl
> bent into the shape of a soothed storm.

How could you have left us with such wind?
Twenty-one and twenty-nine are awfully young
moments of pain far from any sea. The Aegean.
The Ionian. And when not populated,

> their islands breed olive oil
> and grape seed into the wrists of those who wait.
> *He saw the veins of men as a net*
> *the gods made to catch us in like wild beasts,*

Seferis wrote. And still, the agony
of Greece. The way it followed one of you
to Messenia, the other all the way across the ocean,
down the crow's sad throat. Bacteria lurks.

> Pandemics come and go. Think of all
> the dandelions blowing cotton
> into wind coming up from the Gulf.
> One day, we're wind. The next, a piece

of perfect music. Think of monkey bars
children swing on through slush-colored dusk.
Think of lightning bugs coming on
and off as the moon drops coins into the thick

animal night, into their boneless bodies.
If I could live without dying, I would
smoke a pack or two of Luckies a day,
or sit meditating at the foot

of Mount Kailash in the Himalayas?
Who could have known when they entered
their bodies that twenty-one and twenty-nine
would become marks on a stone? That such

bacteria- and virus-free years would be all they would have?
Would I make love like an aspirin
in a glass of water, dissolving into the Belovèd
all the right ways I am woefully wrong?

3.

There are many ways to be wrong. Many
human ways to be born. We come
into these bodies, oddly enough,
as a fleck of fierce flesh, asking that it stay

intact. That our breath be easy. Our eyes
complete. We spill the salt. Kiss the icon.
Beckon the breath of any bit of light
that is unspeakably divine. Ioannis got bit

by bacteria before he even made love
to his first woman, exchanging only
cookies and candied almonds the night before
he left to be stationed at what he did not know

would be his first and final front. Theodorosios
at least got a chance to step the gangways
and storefronts of Chicago's South Side.
Frequent market stalls in ways that said it was time

his father brought the rest of the eight
children over from the Old Country dusk
into the possibility of calmed mouths.
There are many ways to be brought over. Storms

to be averted. Legs to uncross at a funeral.
Slippers placed perfectly upright at bedsides
so that children can be conceived.
Children, we pray, that will assuage

the gods to grant them long lives
and with the coin of their innocence
one day convince Charon to ferry them
to the right side of the river. Dear Ioannis. Belovèd

Theodorosios. Though we never met
before you left the body, I know you
in ways the wind won't. In ways it cuts across
the moon and dangles grassy umbilical cords

that sway but do not break—as the world
bends. There are many ways. Many ways
to be. Human. Paths through which to be. Born.
One is to die so beautifully into your death

that you shame the gods and their fate
away. Another is to die and be
reborn yet again—a century later, perhaps—
through the mouths of your descendants.

Into the glorious grief and restoration of bloodlines
beckoning the tongue back and forth across the page.
What we think might be the uncut possibility
of a poem, or at least a woeful wobbling of words.

Solaki Census Interview with My Great-Grandmother Vasiliki Demopoulos (1862–1954)

I: For the record, please state your full name.
V: Last night, the moon entered—slantwise—my throat.

I: So your name, then, is *Moon*?
V: The priest who came last year from Mount Athos said there are few plants belonging to anyone named *Cave-Dweller*.

I: Okay, then. How about your age? The previous census has you being born in either 1859, 1861, or 1862.
V: Yesterday, I brought a stray cat home and fed it a bowl of goat's milk. How many more lives it has is anyone's guess.

I: The number of children you currently mother?
V: The fingers on my right hand equal those on my left. The fingers on my left hand outnumber those on my right. The sun weighs the same as the moon, even when both are full.

I: Your husband. What is his current profession?
V: We have three mirrors in our house, four of which are very kind to me and show me not a single gray hair.

I: It is my understanding that your husband, Panayiotis, was a teacher and a great orator here in Solaki before departing for the United States. That in his forties he had wanted to become a priest, but politics got involved, and another farmer was chosen instead. Your husband felt insulted and, thus, decided that to better his family he would leave you here in Solaki with eight children while he tried to make a living as a furniture maker, planning to send for you and the children one at a time when he could afford passage to join him in the New World.

V: I'm not sure I hear a question.

I: You were born in Solaki?

V: I was born in Solaki?

I: Yes. That's what I'm asking.

V: Who among us is ever really born? Once I was a cypress tree. Another time, a dandelion root.

I: Ages, please, of each of your eight children.

V: One plus one never equals zero.

I: You seem reluctant to give precise answers.

V: Thank you.

I: No, I wasn't complimenting you. Can I get you some coffee? My wife filled this thermos for me, and she packed a small flask with cream.

V: Thank you.

I: Cream?

V: Thank you is so insufficient a word when we face the wind and lay our troubles down into the moon-bent grass.

I: We should cover your household income.

V: We have two kerosene lamps—with just enough fuel to read by them one hour each night before bed.

I: I see. You practice the Orthodox faith?

V: Yes, of course. And the poems of Dionysios Solomos. The precepts of Pythagoras.

I: How many luxury items—if any—do you own?
V: They say olive oil soap is best to wash with and not eat.

I: Let's keep to numbers.
V: Doesn't every woman have two legs? Two silky armpits?

I: Earlier you mentioned the moon regarding your name.
What did you mean exactly by "entered—slantwise—my
throat"?
V: If I spoke your name at night into moth wings beating
against the lamp, would the pigs in your yard turn into wind
gusts mimicking the bleating of goats?

I: Anything with which you'd like to close? Your husband will
send for you soon?
V: The priest who came last year had a beard as long as a
three-day headache. What are the migration habits of hen-
eels? Odysseus's dog, Argos, remembered what it was like to
be the only one to recognize him upon his return.

Three Angels

based on an icon, Holy Trinity, *painted by Elizabeth Murphy*

1.
No, not just the Archangels Michael, Gabriel,
and Raphael. Or the triadic urge
of God in which the Holy Spirit infuses

both Father and Son with three ways
of mouth. Not even the Hindu Trinity
of Brahma, Vishnu, and Shiva

that Alexander found when he reached the end
of his quest and sat a dusty road
in India, finally turning for home

only after talking long with a holy man
in dhoti. But Elytis, Seferis, and Ritsos,
three corners of a building—the reader,

the fourth. This is not sacrilege. It is never
sacrilege to consume the body and blood
of the poem. We bend. We kneel. We beg

of it our mouths. Each of their words,
how they entered the uncertainty
of my mid-twenties. The luminous Aegean

melancholy of Elytis. Seferis's longing
for perfection, a mermaid on a ship
crucified to the wheel while she was still

beautiful. Ritsos in detention camps, resisting the junta,
then writing *Scripture of the Blind* in just two months
under surveillance in Athens and Kalamos.

2.

Let's say I can't say it right. That I can never   say it
right. That my right word   wobbles.   That it weathers
and   wrongs.   That I pout and   pore. Flatline

the dirge of my own sad   urge. When,   before
the altar,   I take the red communion   cloth
to my   chin.   And the priest sinks his gold

          spoon into the chalice,
asking my name   in Greek. *Giorgos,* I say.   *Giorgos.*
As if a cave in Zakynthos   and my Avgerinos

blood. As if a poverty   of bread   soaked
from the   Kalamarases   in Pharaklatha.
          The Demopouloses   in Solaki.

As if Mount Athos   and the silence residing inside
centuries of   meditation. And the priest   prays,
sliding the body and blood   the body

and the blood   of the poem   onto the torn
          of my tongue. Brahma. Vishnu. Shiva.
Three corners   of a mouth remaking itself,

          reaching
into the next   world

where the duality   of two   is not enough. Is *never*

enough.   Even St. George
rides his glorious white   horse   down
                the depths

of my throat,   searching for   words.
Oh, how I love   the   words
inside the   words. The howl   of a pure and lasting

vowel. The animal   in my tongue. The poem inside
the darkening   light
of a moon-drenched   day. A day

of absolute   Aegean   melancholy
in which Elytis drops   deadfalls   of light,
                mantra-like,

into my right   and wrangled ear. A day
        in which   Seferis bone-blurs
my word   as the Parthenon breaks

yet   retains   crumbling
stones. Ritsos urging me   to drench my moon-dark sleep
within the eyes   of the clinically deaf.

3.
Once—I must confide—when I was alive, I was
dead. Once, when I died, I came back
again and again. Into a body.

A *human* body. Each time, distinct. A monk, say,
from Mount Athos. A moon worshipper eating a locust
in the Kalahari. A yogi in Banaras smeared in ash,

meditating on cremation grounds on the banks
of Mother Ganga. Even a Tantric vowel
in the mouths of the moon-soaked

and the many-dead. No, not the saintly wind
of three Archangels—Michael, Gabriel, and Raphael.
Or the many gods bridging East and West, almost

always coming in threes. Not even the shaman's three toes
crossed at birth. Or the three-directional horns of the aurochs
painted in ibex blood on cave walls in Lascaux.

But Elytis, Seferis, and Ritsos. There, in this book
or that, forty years ago waiting
for my wobbling words to be born

unto them, to speak their poems from inside
the ash-smeared crevices of my *own* mouth. Where I've sat
many years with the Orphic weight of a stone.

And I sink into the cave places—huts in the Himalayas,
thickets in Yunnan, even seaside holes housing dead but living
scrolls. And the places, the cave places into which

I sink. Where the poem bends into me,
making my mouth. The sound of a vowel
like moaning from the mouths of the dead.

The sound of a lamb tongue unrolling in my chest
the sacred dust of the sea: Elytis, Seferis, Ritsos.
Blessèd be the poem. *Blessèd be the poem.* The poem

we grow. The poem that grows *us*. That grows *into* us
and through. The poem we had not known
would bless and—in blessing us—be most blessèd.

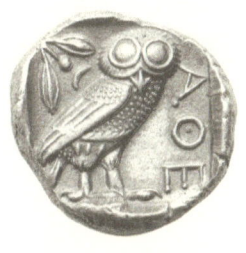

NINE

What We Speak Speaks Us

On Prison and Holy Hashish: Elias Petropoulos,
    the *Enfant Terrible* of Modern Greek Letters

> *And I said to my wife:*
> *—when I die like a dog here in Paris,*
> *burn my corpse in the crematorium*
> *then toss the ashes into a sewer.*
> *This is my testament.*
>   —Elias Petropoulos

You are dead in the way
a boy's hair turns green.

You piss on the ruins
of Rhodes, and part of your mouth

becomes pus of the moon.
Cypress trees bow when your name

bows down into them. Vassilis Tsitsanis
keeps waiting for you with his bouzouki,

bringing you into the underworld
of *rembetika*—prostitutes, homosexuals,

hash smokers, and petty thieves. Horses
of the junta keep tracking you with their iron

hooves. The Colonels clean their teeth
with a pick, swearing you are still there

somewhere inside. Even after three different
jail sentences. Your common-law wife weeps

when your breath finally moves from the body
burdening the cot into a Eurasian nightjar.

Once again, she pours your ashes—as you
requested—into a sewer in France.

Rita Boumi-Pappas Confronts Stalin, Finally, in a Dream

If I go out walking with my dead friends
—Rita Boumi-Pappas

Heterogeneous branches of the tongue crowned in shadows
of dirt and poor. The murmuring of trees burned you.

You wrote about the wages of bread crusts
soaked in a bit of spoiled milk. Wrote

about those who could not afford time in a living
forest. You wrote "The Crow" in homage

to Stalin. Asked your teeth when they hurt
if they could bite you. Instead. The dog you longed

to hold was a thin, pale cat sprawled on a rummaged Asian
rug. All the patterns of the poor infuriated you.

They clocked on and on for centuries. Filled you
with bus fumes from the cities in which you hid,

diverse as Athens, Sofia, and East Berlin. Now you see
the bird buried in salt. Now you don't. The salt pleads

through you. Discarded cardboard boxes make a home
for the not-yet-dead. You call the archangel of the State

down into your mouth, where the Black Sea and the Baltic
exchange scrapings of dead fish scales into your sleep.

I beg. Beg you, Rita. Clothe your eyes. Step aside. Don't drink.

Costas Yiannoulopoulos Tunes His Radio
to the Dusky Voice of Mangroves

If we look sideways through our throats,
you are there, from your radio show, tapping your foot

to the riffs and licks of Charles Mingus. Tune your radio
receiver to the voice of mangroves scraping the night loose

from their skin. Yes, it resembles the sound of casualties
from the Greek Civil War. That's one reason you gave us

jazz, Costas. And one reason *skin* and *sin* part ways
over a single letter the way water bends

around river rock. Then merges again on the other side
as something whole. What are the zodiac

moods of Mingus, Monk, and Miles? A horoscope
of milk descends from their fingers. An exile

you heard all the way home to Peireas from Alexandria.
It has been written that you first came to sound, Costas,

in the startlings of the womb. When you emerged,
fractured, you hoped to reclaim your warm embrace of bees.

A locomotive is one way to travel into eternity,
especially when hearing its distance stun the night

while you darn a sock? Water in the shape
of water makes the sound of Mingus

unscrewing his shoes and placing them in your throat?
You stepped there, leaving hyena tracks in mud,

fleas flaring your nostrils, as you translated Ferlinghetti,
Brautigan, and Corso. And the bend from plane trees

in Aegean wind is something you knew we needed to hear
so our inner sound would not subside. So that war

would stop taking the shape of war. Something
sedimentary, brackish, from as far away as the coast of Borneo,

seawater crawling out into the root tangles we survive.
Costas Yiannoulopoulos, you brought a threatening sky

into the lives of the tamarind and the tamed. You soothe
yet sooth. In your Lee Morgan. In your Kenny Dorham

way. Exhume musical notes. Each a fragment
of *skin* that *sins*. Sometimes the difference between two words

is difficult to discern. Sometimes the sound of both
moves around stones, even as they rearrange the stones.

Roots, at times, snarl even the knots that tangle them.
In sorrow. In song. In the jazz patterns

connecting Athens to New Guinea. Lanterns
in the rich mineral rinse of the locomotive night

pierce the mountain-pass dark, rearranging the dark
like your late-night jazz radio throat, Costas, telling

the world *to* the world the way the world should be.

A Reading from the Epistle of Nikos Engonopoulos

So, I was born within
    the folds of a mountain pine,
        inside the shadowy cloak

of a crow. My belovèd brothers
    in Breton. Sisters in Soupault
        and Desnos. I implore you, speak

unto the tongue as if you *were*
    the tongue. Its quagmire
        and quick. And all the rancor

of beautifully disturbed bees.
    For I am with you, here, within
        the juxtaposition of an umbrella

and the tragus of my left
    ear. I am with you, belovèd
        Athenians, as if what we speak

speaks *us*, just in the act
    of listening. To the sound
        of a steam-driven train

from Magritte's chimney,
    I say unto thee, let there be an outside
        to every inner sound, to the whingeing

wind when we rise
    from a blood-terraced dream
        and find in the sudden found

death among the rows
    of grapes we might smoosh into
        wine. A fierce, falconed olive

pit keeps
    churning our tongue
        into the night soil

nurturing a philodendron.
    Philo, of course, means love,
        though in the language

of wasps it might be a fierce
    stinging that guides our mouths
        back among our maculate

hands. Hand me the salt
    Delvaux dredged up
        from the Ionian Sea

and placed among his blank-
    faced women whose distant
        pout painted him into a constant

gesso-scraping for more.
    My brothers in Perét. My sisters
        in the deathbed dirge of René Daumal.

I beg of you and ask of it and cry
    unto thee. Here in the high pines.
        There, from inside the crow's calm,

I speak what speaks me, in pine sleeves
    and wind hollows. In the ever-
        shifting words that are my name.

D. I. Antoniou and the Nostalgia for Distant Places

You are going to suffer again
playing with poetry;
it's like a medicine:
you should know the dosage,
to find the cure for poison.
                  —Dimitris Antoniou

He sailed beyond the genius
of what he sang. He hunted the moon
he knew was lodged, somewhere,
in his throat.

            There were sunsets, and there
were languages drowning in the four corners
of the earth. In Eliot. In Stevens. In the way
George Seferis translated their chthonic

bees. Solitude, say, in the sea's bewitching
sting sunk in casks of distant suns the ocean
swallowed. D. I. Antoniou spent his years
adrift, moving from this port to that. Yes, he came

from a seafaring family, was a captain himself, the whole
of him, dispersed like a climate of trees calming down
a declaration of wind-scruff and Self. When he sailed
into the Black Sea he became waves

of the sea's dark loops. When he moved through
his glowing own Mediterranean, the Ionian Sea rose
in this throat, stirring months-long mud resin. Seed.
An urge to never seek firm land. Those nights alone,

anchored in his ship's cabin, moon-ache burning
the back of his throat, he wrote his life
by kerosene lamp. Kerosene lamp
that flickered waves of the way

the world tossed him through the unending
rise and fall of the sea's froth. What genius, the sea,
singing him almost whole as he sang it back
beyond the idea of order, of *moving, always keep*

moving. There are magnets of loneliness, he knew,
that keep expelling one into exile. From land. Wind.
From coconut palms whose curvy brown bend
kept him believing the sea and what it sang

was all it could possibly be. If it was the sea itself
and not the merchant marines that lured him on
like a syllable he recognized only in the silence after
he spoke. A syllable lost among the waves, the reeds.

George Vafopoulos Contemplates the Sea
Below His Tongue

Time, he knew, stood running. Still,
it seemed, he held a jellyfish in his mouth.

A stingray from the coral reefs of the Aegean.
There, very near his tonsils. Primordial time

nourishing, perplexing, his words. Diced cubes
of sea cucumber he consulted as an oracle,

knowing the Orthodox faith
and the wisdom of Mount Athos

were part of the wind that was part
of the trees that seemed to be part of the everlasting

sea grass. Everyone seemed to know Ritsos
was a Red. Theodorakis too. That was fine, he thought.

But what color in the midnight dark, he wondered, was he,
George Vafopoulos, when he waded this way, that—

knee-deep in his own mouth? Was he Aegean
blue? Parthenon white? The trembling

sea-cucumber green of the cross troubling the waves
of the Greek flag? Color was mischievous. Was always

changing shades in sparkling sea light. Could account
for the way his mouth. For the way his mouth

started. Stopped. And mimicked, sometimes,
a startling rain battering the beach.

His month on Holy Mount Athos meant more
to him than that recurring dream of lobsters and squids

guiding him to a chamber where perplexity dissolved.
Than his sudden beard, say, some mornings,

whenever he wrote a poem about a ship or the wind or sea
anemones flowering his brain. Whenever, in the narthex

of the church, he lit a candle before the icon of Nicholas,
seafarer saint. This was the world that was below his tongue.

This, the world, of Athos. Surrounded by sea, by creatures
he could not quite name. A world that might allow the night

sounds of stars crushing into themselves.
That nightly repaired itself, even as it tore

itself apart. He was convinced that if he got the words
just right that the jellyfish swimming there

below his tongue might stop stinging him.
And with their gelatinous, medusa-phase

bodies bring back the dance of the dead
in one translucent streak. Telling.

Telling him what and where
he had been. Been before

he had been forgotten. Had forgotten
the sea and all he had borne in being born.

Thoreau Studies Classical Greek So Long, He Wakes One Morning Only to See Homer in His Mirror

I went to the sea because I wished to sail deliberately, and not, when I came to die, discover never having ever truly drowned.

Even ships do not crash against the rocks without a groan.

I have set sail inside my own blood. Inside the wind inside my blood.

Disobedience is the true foundation of liberty. The use of Theban slaves as oarsmen must be the intractably compliant idea that forced labor resembles the possibility that the moon invoking a wooded cabin might actually *not* calm the sea.

In other words, a man is rich in proportion to the number of Trojans he can kill.

Yesterday, Sappho's falcon flew slantwise through my throat. And Walden Pond will always be just one drainage ditch into which the Aegean empties.

Live, I tell you, the life Pericles on his throne imagined for himself.

Or die of pneumonia like Alexander only after having reached India and realizing he should have stayed home by the log fire with the sound of wind and a dear devoted dog.

In fact, our truest life is when we are in dreams awake.

Concord, Massachusetts, a crowd of people stuck as the helots of Sparta.

The mass of men, I tell you, lead lives.

The mass of lives end up, in the end, quite desperately dead.

I have set sail quietly inside my own saliva. Even within this beard which refuses splintered shavings of a morning rain. To return each chin hair home after a ten-year war.

When I tutored the children of Emerson in classical Greek, I extracted three fingers of salt from the Trojan gods with which to pepper the young ones' brains.

Kabir says, *Go to the inner woods to learn from trees to breathe*; Homer says, *Cut down the trees around the secluded pond—even on the slopes of wooded Zakynthos—and build a new ship so you can flee to the sea.*

Lafcadio Hearn Dreams That He Will Be Reborn Eleven Years After His Death in the Body of Thomas Merton

I am a Russian fish owl embroiled in the chest of night on the eastern coast near the Sea of Japan.

If the moon were not a kerosene rag, then the mice would not lament.

For many years, I lived inside a Kyoto teahouse (no, not as some say, inside a shamisen plucked in a brothel).

My Greek mother has—for many years now—become a cup of Gyokuro tea.

If the rain were porcelain, it would be her.

I would like to say how much it hurts to drink starlight through the foreheads of the dead.

Winters in the primeval forest still snow inside me.

There are dreams of American monks and *Asian Journals* and electric cords we tell no one.

I was shocked into this life, named Πατρίκιος Λευκάδιος Χερν, on the island of Lefkada in 1850.

This is what happens when you spend decades collecting ghost stories and taking a Japanese wife.

This is what occurs when they call you Koizumi Yakumo, beautifully written as, 小泉 八雲

Some pictures draw us. Draw us further into their slopes of shivering red. Of shivering red cedars.

There are gorges lined with conifers and swamps full of mice.

I swear—for some inexplicable reason I believe we should all avoid Bangkok fans and afternoon naps and wire cords.

What we dream will one day dream us—whether we coax it beneath a full moon or near the end of a meridian nap.

I have never been to Kentucky or even Fort Wayne, Indiana, except as a ghost voice impinging the thick skin of the sycamores.

What the wind winds through blows one soul into another.

I met a famous haiku poet last week, seated in his sparse two-tatami mat cell, who warned me never to use the word *soul* in a poem. *Boil the image down into the rarely glimpsed largest known owl in the world,* he advised.

I bow to the feathers of my Greek Icarus blood that have brought me this far.

I bow to the rocks of life, waiting below—splashed with sea salt and rain—that long to quarter me.

I bow to the dawn temple bells in Kyoto. Their breaking bows to *me*.

Takis Sinopoulos and the Sound That Is Heard

hearing the sound that is heard
—Takis Sinopoulos

Somehow he had become the eardrum
of a lightning bug. Silence existed
as a mountain of naked medicine. Each morning
Takis Sinopoulos sipped poison from the poised slipper,
points from the darts stiffening
his shirt collar. He remembered, years
before, his comrades on the front,
scouring their own blood
for some answer: a lost leg, the finger
that became the example, sixteen inches
of startled intestines. Codeine. Quinine.
Morphine. Like an infant about to be given
suck. Like the crush of a temple bell
reminding him it was too late.

*

Wings are what he wanted, what he listened for in his lungs.
In his esophagus. In what was left of his heart. Are what he
tested for in others, even now, as a general practitioner in
Athens. *Cavafy would know*, Takis Sinopoulos mused. And
he investigated a stain on his sheet that somehow smelled of
Alexandria and inkwells of sea salt and nights of desperation
without loving. *Ritsos, too, would understand*, he reasoned,
holding the stethoscope up to his own bronchial tubes.
His own complicated heart. Feeling the chill that gave him
gooseflesh. Even turning his head slightly to the left, forcing

a cough. And something like a poison dart parted the fifth
rib on his left side. Blood and water, what St. John saw that
afternoon at Golgotha and was the only one of the Four
Evangelists to cite the mixture and unintentionally coax it
centuries later into the Holy Mass.

*

Each morning, yes, each morning a mountain
of salient meditation grew in Takis Sinopoulos

like troubled and discarded salt. He heard voices.
Kept hearing voices. From his war-torn core. Petros Kallinikos:

My arm! Oh, God, where's my arm! Lieutenant Nikos Poulios:
Doctor Takis, it hurts whenever I breathe, and all I see

when I try to sleep is that mule blown to bits by its own load
of dynamite, and the crush of gravel, and my men—

Blessèd Virgin!—my men. Even some soldier with amnesia
who knew himself only as Lefteris: *My intestines?*

Was it my own intestines I crawled into, as I dragged them
and myself from Thessaloniki all the way to the moon?

*

Somehow, for a moment, Takis heard dissolve, *was* dissolve,
and dispersed throughout his entire inner ear. Sudden fields
of goldenrod dampening during the dark. Drench of evening
corpses drying out. The repetitive splash of moon pouring

through him, lighting his wingèd body periodically among
the gnats. But always the stirrup stir and return to the
Occupation's beat beat beat of Wagner's invisible baton and
Icarus's final cry among the rocks. To the pulsing aftermath
of the body programmed to hang on no matter what, from
the moment the sperm and ovum unite and form the medulla
oblongata, to the forced breath of the brain-dead.

*

Each morning,   yes,   a mound of solvent
blew into Takis Sinopoulos's left   ear. Crush of an infant
about to be given suck.   Eardrum of a man   of height
and sun,   pitch and   salt. *I am hearing the sound
that is heard*, he'd think. Sound,   yes,   the sound
that is   heard: sudden buckshot of   sparrows
in a lieutenant's belly,   grating of a crow's feather
fashioned into a child's   arm,   rustling
prostheses of wings   attached to the backs
of all those   who after the war   wanted to
but could not.   Die. This troubled him. *Everything* troubled him.
          Tongue depressor, stethoscope,
hemostat,   physician's touch.   Even today,
St. John's Day,   the day after   Epiphany. Blood
          and a drop of water
on his physician gauze, soaking   through   onto
the table. The pregnant woman,   eight months,
legs spread   on the table before him—   *Blessèd Virgin!*
he exclaims. *Is that an arm in there?*   *A wing?*
                    Or a stick   *of dynamite?*

216

Jenny Mastoraki and the Multiple Mounds of Hurt

Her poems are badger dens disguised
as *Stop. Wait. Listen.* Among us move
the many murders of Jenny Mastoraki. Her words.
Her way of mouth. The many blows military batons
beat, battering her almost into another life. Wind comes
as all winds do. As do death and the after-
bath of a pummeled body left to hemorrhage
on the stone steps of the University of Athens
library. One baton-pop. Two. This rib,
that. Count the splinters. Scour the badger dens
for the number of termites
multiple in the mounds. God, no!
How high can the concussive count?

Some say we hold in the belly the *birth*
of the belly. Some say, no, there are Aegean sails
sent forth from there to find Ithaca,
even the Golden Fleece. Yet all agree,
what's in the belly is never expelled. Completely.

And it cries out, this belly-
urge. Roped against the mast
of the body, begging to flee the duodenum
for the *pharmakeia* of Circe.

Like love, say, or anger. Transformed
into lions. Wolves. Swine. Or into the memory of Jenny
on a stone step, reciting her poems courageously against
a military coup. Brave and fierce as the wind
Odysseus longed to listen to and begged
his men to let him become.

Jack Spicer Encounters Dimitris Papaditsas,
    Believing the Voice He Hears Late at Night
    Is a Radio Wave from Mars

*Toenail clippings. Horsehair shirts. Monks from Mount Athos
carrying stones in their mouths.*

These things, Jack Spicer heard one night, lying in bed,
unable to sleep, tuning his inner radio receiver to Mars.

Papaditsas was still alive, somehow broadcasting stray
thoughts across the ocean as he meditated upon the Surrealist
paintings of Nikos Engonopoulos and Giorgos Vakalo.

*When one drinks a cup of tea, the moon is pouring the sad salt
of Greece through its glandular curve. Here, spit into my mouth,
and we will be one with an iguana lolling on a rock in the
Galápagos.*

Phrases like this puzzled Spicer. As he tossed his bed. And
turned. Linguist that he was, heartfelt of Old English vowels,
he knew Beowulf would never speak such atrocities, engaged
as he was in fighting Grendel.

Or were these fragments of conversations—half-heard in
booths he passed on the way to the can? Leftover bar talk
from Gino & Carlo's? From Enrico's? Maybe from Plaka
Taverna, on Kearny near Broadway, where you could down
shots of *ouzo*, hear bouzouki music, and break a plate?

Words puzzled him. Jigsaw puzzles too. Why should a picture be fractured? A word? And all that transmigration. The olives, grape leaves, and wine of the Greek myths somehow becoming the peas and parsnips of Old English epics. Cabbage and wild boar filling the Anglo Saxons with lust.

We are all dusting into one another, even while alive, the unknown voice that was Papaditsas seemed to say, though through the static it was hard to tell. *Like André Breton and Robert Desnos flaking into one another,* it continued. *Why do you think termites build mounds against atrocities in French Equatorial Africa, in Ubangi-Shari, when the rains have ceased?*

Of course, such words were disconcerting. Spicer took them to Robert Duncan. To Jess. To Helen Adam. George Stanley. Robin Blaser. And Ebbe Beauregard. Even to what he took to be a falconress, who seemed to preen herself and suggest all answers could be found while digging meticulously into oneself, nudging most ectoparasites away. *We must study Lorca,* he realized, telling each of his friends in turn. *As a way to decode what of our mouths our ears most want to grant.*

And it went on like this for weeks. Months. And more months. Jack unable to sleep. Hearing Papaditsas disguising the dark. Dispatching Surrealist reports. Into the dusky parts of Spicer's brain—half asleep, half awake, the third half unable to do math.

Look, he heard, just before the visitations ceased, *there is a sirocco coming into my body here in Athens, all the way from*

Arabia. But it is not dust or tobacco fragments from the warm winds entering me; it is bees swarming from your own backyard. Listen carefully to the sound of your tongue, Jack, absorbing water from wind from out of the soft center of bread. Your broken body there in your own sad mouth, the voice continued. *The mouth of Greece crawling out to you night after night from a time before. Into your one-too-many drinks. Into the restless edge of your lexicon. The say-so-yes-no / right-way-wrong. In the muddled ecstasy of your time of mouth. In your time of what used to be. Most sound. Sleep.*

Apparently Hector Kaknavatos

with a first line by Kaknavatos

Apparently it could not be otherwise
Apparently the kerosene lamps had been set in your chest
Apparently even your mathematics could not save you
And the onslaught of the junta tore your tongue
You looked in the mirror and saw a land of blood and hooks
You were Chiron, the superlative centaur, the wounded healer
If the wind in your throat had not been blood
If the blood nets had not been lowered into the sea
If your chest had not been a crowded school of trapped fish
Apparently, though, it was
Apparently it could not be otherwise
Apparently when it tried to be, even your chest was only half
Half horse half man the third half an unpunctuated phrase
Leave the commas aside, you pleaded, *Allow the world its mouth*
The last instant recanted, including the pauses most needed
Otherwise, it could apparently not be
Not apparently could it otherwise
Not in Oulipo and its mathematical madness
You turned to Surrealism you turned to myth
You were the son of Titan Cronus and the sea nymph Philyra
How could your body have been half horse?
Your poems, Hector, had *grown* hoarse among the Colonels'
Manly stance
You were smart to hide your mustache
To clean your ears with tobacco leaves, to clone your toes
You stood against the wind crowding your owl
And the forest on fire in the kitchen sink
Apparently it could not be otherwise
Apparently your Surrealism would have lodged in their throats

Declared you decoded of letters not to be trusted
Declared you once and for maybe
You were named for a Trojan prince, greatest warrior of Troy
You were said to have killed 31,000 Greek warriors
You—Hector—could only be killed by Achilles himself
What rose in him, centuries before, from heel to heart?
What caused you to be reborn half horse, half man?
To be reborn in 1920 as Hector Kaknavatos, the poet?
You have largely and not, mostly and more
You have mostly not been forgotten even when you have
You have lit the kerosene lamps in the watery chests of fish
Known the sea because a sea nymph gave you suck
You called her *Mother* you called her *Phrase Without a Pause*
You knew the enchantment of lamps the burning word
The wick the match we carry inside
In our mouths is housed the beginning of all sound
The ear and vowel lodging of pain in the loud of the mouth
O Hector, O Kaknavatos
O Ektor, spelled the ancient way as a tunneling within
You have been waiting for the poem to mouth you into sound
You have been waiting in our land of far too few—and words
Below ground the pound of the indignant sea
Below ground your casket and its sway
Apparently it could not be otherwise
Apparently it could not be
Apparently it could and couldn't and maybe still can't
Like all things Surrealist
The fortuitous meeting of Hector, Achilles, and an umbrella
The chance of horse and man on the dissecting table
Like you Hector Kaknavatos
Like your mathematics disguised in the tamp of a lamp
Where your voice wisely hid those years from the Colonels
So that you could be with us now and forever
Hector Kaknavatos's word without end—again

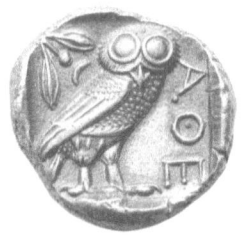

TEN

For My Family

To Absorb the Wind

There was a crow trying to fly through
the darkness of my body. Three cows
in the pasture looked up into what they thought
was nothing but blurred air.

Indiana oaks and maples bent their way back
through me. With a wind stirred forty-five minutes
southwest. *A tornado was spotted just outside
Kankakee*, we heard through the fizz and hiss
of radio static. And we lit candles
in the basement before the icon of St. George.

Now, the sky turns a pale anemic green.
I turn to the poems of René Daumal, grateful
for pataphysics, for the imaginary
solution of water forsaking water. For stairwells
steep with sleep. For my lungs not housing consumption
like his had. I light a candle
and place it on my chest—the white horse
of my chest—lying down to absorb
the wind and all its aching.

Yes, my family taught me what it means
to be Greek. Whenever I stand by a river
or swamp, I watch for wind in the trees
and imagine the boat ride and all the ripples
across. All the names on the ship's log
like ancient cities. Abandoned. Befuddled
battles, rueful and bruised. Like exotic diseases
I struggle to pronounce. One death dying.
One death beckoning another.

Essais

Once, when I was a child king, the world seemed
a bit smaller. Or perhaps larger. Regret
arose from those we loved, remnants of hurts
they'd had with others before we'd met. And the fire ants
of Namibia embedded themselves in my then-young
wrist. Only to lodge there and become something
like lifelong pets. It wasn't Mesopotamia and the fertile regions
of the brain. It wasn't a tornado, found in the gangway
in Chicago where ghosts had roamed. It wasn't the way
flames of the fire in the hearth would rise and fall
without any seeming book being read
into them. I loved the words of Lord Byron.
The way he gave of himself to a cause
made my unmade bed seem all the more sad.
The stitch in my tongue, a calming salve. And Seferis
came to soothe the eyelid twitch that arrived
nights, alone, without me even knowing.
Part of the history of my family made me
read Nikos Gatsos deeply to uncover whatever hope there was
in loss, as he bet the dice again and again and gambled away
even the copyright to his popular songs.

                                       I don't have
a better way to bend my knee and beg forgiveness.
Mostly from myself. For the time wasted reading

unsolved detective novels, especially
the unfinished one Jack Spicer wrote in the 1950s
and that I've read four times, maybe five, knowing each time
there would be no end. I thought *The Tower of Babel*
was just a book. Maybe a metaphor connecting our past
to our unresolved future. It's not doubletalk
when we consider the literal Tower of Babel and the workers'
confusion as they tried to build a world touching heaven.
What was the gift of being born into a family of immigrant
Greeks, I'd wondered—words from my grandfather's island
mixed in, as seasoning, with school and Indiana
history? What was it like for modern Greek poets
to write in Demotic rather than in the formal
Katharevousa? What parts of their tongue did they risk—
Elytis, when he spoke the accents of the heavens? Ritsos,
the stresses of the streets? Embirikos, when he tunneled into
the Bretonian tongue heretofore too much ignored? Even
Elias Petropoulos, the *Enfant Terrible* of Modern Greek
Letters, when he included gay slang and underworld
drug talk during the repressive reign of the Colonels?

I want to remind the world that he received
three prison sentences in seven years. How each trial
found him guilty. How his essays became an anthropology
of the dead. How he was the only Greek
during the seven-year dictatorship to be bold enough
to defy the junta and its mandatory religious beliefs
by listing *atheist* on his identity card. How among his peers
he was the only one who kept a burnt owl in his chest.
I want to remind my family that they spoke me
awake, even when broken. And I walk their rainy

Athenian vowels, still, as if they are Paris streets leading
to the dark parts of my heart that are certain to heal.

These are the things that don't add up, even when they join
brick to brick in the existing tower my words have long
built to pierce the clouds and try to harmonize
the sky. Especially the clouds of Indiana
with the mountains of Zakynthos, Pharaklatha,
and Solaki that keep attempting to reach
into them. I'm not sure I understand all the words
inscribed in the bones of the dead
or the treatises proffering the anthropology of belief.
I'm not sure I have a better way to say
the way different tongues come together—when talking,
when kissing, when gently nudging the tender places
our bodies nest as if composed entirely of birds.

Bird of heaven, burning cloud in the cavilings of the chest,
I love you, even when you're fleeing. Even when the rains
cease and you're bringing back to the Ark
an olive leaf from dry land. Even when
you're cooing over my two or more ways
of mouth—the Old Country and the New.
Or over two exiles, say, who settled in Paris
to escape the sway of the regime. When you're poised
on a telephone pole—lovely dove—observing
Elias Petropoulos's common-law wife as she weeps the streets
of France at his passing and opens a grate, pouring—
as his last request—his ashes into a sewer.

Homage to Konstantina

for my great-grandmother Konstantina Kalamaras,
(dates unknown), born Konstantina Georgopoulos

Great-grandmother.
You remain a mountain
pass in Pharaklatha.

Your bones slow
your matutinal fire
down into
the Achelous River.
Into the Maritsa. The Thyamis.
All the way to the Aegean.

Great-grandmother. I trace you
in my Kalamaras blood. My
Georgopoulos blood. I taste you
in the night
air. Here, in Indiana.
Its runnels and rills. Savor you,
Konstantina, in the lightning
bugs' embrace.
In the midnight movement
of mayflies
over the Maumee.
In drops of moonlight
into which I dip
my cup tonight
and lift,
tenderly,
from the well.

Journey from Nemnitsa in Kyparissia

*for my great-great-grandfather Panagiotis Kalamaras,
1780–1861—and for my great-great-grandmother,
whose name and dates (of birth and death) remain
unknown*

Thus, the Angel spoke unto me,
saying I was thrown from the loins
of Panagiotis Kalamaras, unto whom was given
six sons—my great-grandfather Pericles
and his five brothers, Vasilios, Pantelis, Giorgos,
Demetrios, and Michalis.

And it was spoken unto, *into*, me
that my great-great-grandmother—nameless,
her birth and death dates unknown—gave birth
to each son on a small cot
in their home in the village of Nemnitsa,
no longer even called that. Changed, now,
to Methydrion.

And the Angel handed me poems stitched
into goatskin, the words, the rhythms
of George Seferis. Of Odysseus Elytis.
Of Yannis Ritsos. Reminding me
that I'd been born a Kalamaras in a riverbed
in Nemnitsa—sucking the milk
of a she-goat—already able to read
at birth. That right from the womb,
I could speak as if I had been spoken
into. That I was born from the coupling

of a river and a willow. That of my many moods
I quickly settled on Elytis's "Aegean Melancholy."
That when I started crawling, like a compass point
I sought the island of Samos where Ritsos had been
exiled. Then I sought Athens and Kalamos
where, under surveillance, he wrote *Scripture of the Blind*.
And when looked at lovingly into my milky
eyes, when asked baby questions with cooing
oohs and *aahs*, my response was quick, definite,
fixed. I sadly mouthed from memory the close
of Seferis's "Helen,"
that so much suffering, so much life,
went into the abyss
all for an empty tunic, all for a Helen.

Thus, the Angel tried to console me. She brought
nail clippings. Toy soldiers. A top that spun always
true north. A tiny photo of the sparkling
sea in which I'd once swam
as an octopus. Laboratory slides revealing millennia
in which I'd even been an amoeba. Saying
these are the things I have brought with me many times
into a new body. She lay her long hair
unto me, over me. *In and through.*
And the Orphic bone that became my tongue
had no head to cut off. No Furies to cast it away.
And the Golden Fleece the Angel swaddled me in
had finally been found and brought safely home.
And the Cyclops closed his massive eye, dandling me
on his lap. And the wooden horse
the Angel rolled into my belly opened.
And from inside my own belly, I somehow
tunneled further in, stepping into the horse.

These are the things you may not yet quite understand,
she said unto me. I lay, sleeping
in the horse's belly, which was also somehow
sleeping inside my own. Waiting to emerge
in the dark's dark to seize the City of Troy
I was told was also inside me
295 sea miles from Sparta. Which was there,
too, inside.

Dear Angel of Pharaklatha in Kyparissia—
where the six sons of my great-great-grandfather
Panagiotis had moved from Nemnitsa
upon his death—teach me the name
of my great-great-grandmother. Seemingly lost.
A name muddled in the stones, thrown among all
the ships wrecked upon rocks. A name
the ancient ruins have claimed. A name that Panagiotis
surely must have whispered into her
ear each time they breathed the trees and touched
the moon and created a son.

                        Show me,
Belovèd Angel, the tiny cot. The birthing
rug. The stains of heaven
upon it when I dropped from the starlight
of womb water many decades later
through those who came directly from her.
Lanterns licking the night. Olive oil
the midwife smeared on my great-great-grandmother's
tender places to ease the coming from the dark. The birth-
blood that entered the world before me. Dense,
brightly lit. All the blood. The years. All the decades
of death, dark, and the goodness of delight.
O Belovèd, all we call human,
all for an empty tunic, all for a Helen.

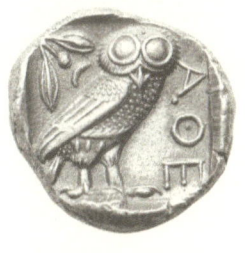

ELEVEN

A Crush of Bees
in Which to Bury the Tongue

Zephy Dharaki Becomes the Moon Becoming a Bee

And so it was told unto the throat
And so the *happy blood of the moment*
She wrote about burst upon a star
And so the blood the star the stars
And all manner of things
Awakened
Zephy Dharaki carried the stone steps of her library
On her back after being fired
In the wake of the coup
She wandered it wandered we wander
Conjugate the complexities of grief
If you dare
Look directly into the eclipse
Of one burning dog eating another watery one
There are special glasses to see such things
Advised for our legs our feet
To cross borders when necessary
Like Antonio Machado fleeing Franco's Spain
Crossing the mountains in a car with his mother on his lap
Zephy Dharaki became the moon becoming a bee
The bee becoming each word each phrase
She piled and layered upon each other into her poems
Happy blood of the moment
She assured us
Blood pouring blood pouring blood
Happy blood of the bee in the throat
And we begged of it to speak to see to one day hear
As we slit our veins on each word
Each phrase
Each storm given us
Each lathering swarm of the holy work

Christos Anesti, Andreas Embirikos

1.

Spear-slit in the bark. Phosphorus. A woman across the street
raised her left arm, felt the tenderness of hair-stubble as a
persistent brush fire. Umbilical phosphorus born in Brăila,
Romania, August 20, 1901 (by the Julian calendar). Or was
it September 2 (by the Gregorian)? Stones in their mouths,
priests from Mount Athos filed by, a throng of smoke. *A crush
of bees is all I want*, thought Andreas Embirikos, *a moment to
bury my tongue beneath her arm, taste the pit of a thousand stars
exiled as scars*. He was a swarm of stars brought, omphalic,
to Greece, melded in Bretonian Paris, spilling out again in
Athens as blood and water onto the cot.

2.

Just a week before, the gardener had axed his own humming
clear out of his spine, beating the woodpile to pulp. Had
since devoted his days to coffee, cigarettes, and bawdy jokes
at the corner *kafeneio*. Now he was gone. Embirikos only saw
empty tables under the incendiary olives begging for silver
tongues to sponge them dry. Never knowing why he was the
first Greek Surrealist, he thirsted for humming, drank coffee
with *ouzo* and honey. A chessboard, carved in Romania on
August 20 (or was it September 2?), on one chair, rusting.
Which calendar, after all, could be thrushed with a handful
of trust? Bees groaning from numerical shiver to numerical
shiver? The chessboard's two missing pieces made a painful
scraping. Wind from Cephalonia coated the throat of a dog
barking back at what it took for a ghost. A match in his left

hand, Embirikos asked, *Is the scar a woman carries in the pit of her arm the cord's blood-light after she buries the afterbirth? Or is it the cord itself?*

3.

Phosphorus of boy-stubble brought in infancy to Athens, moiling out as bright divine death on some August 5 or other. Stone in his mouth, a monk from Mount Athos coiled a long way from his cell onto the cobblestone, signaling a celibate shame. *A handful of bees spilling out of his ear*, repeated Embirikos, watching the monk. *To marry my tongue to her flesh-driven scent.* Sumptuous star exiled among a thousand burning scars, Easter itself arrived as a strand of hair left on a table at the abandoned *kafeneio. The Colonels have come, have stomped out even the desire to sniff the camphor in the tender of your Belovèd's sweat*, he said.

4.

The dog continued to scratch. Only a King and Queen not engaged in coitus could make a pain of such scraping. Wind or ghost? Wing or breath-lamp? Was it any wonder Easter came that year as *both* May 4 and March 30? That it couldn't decide whether it was Julian or Gregorian? Whether it, itself, wanted to die? Sometimes Greek, other times Romanian?

5.

Christos Anesti, he thought—both believing and not that *Christ had risen.* None of it matters—not the purple robe,

not the hair-stubble around her secret underarm scar, not
the spear-slit in the dark where someone continually strikes
a match against the gauze of another's cheek. He recalled the
scent of flesh, the sulfur of military leather, that stone he kept
under his tongue since the Colonels had come. The threat of
a decree hidden in an epaulet. Even the woodcutter poured
arsenic a week earlier onto the lilies—causing a ruckus of bees
in his throat, in Andreas Embirikos's Surrealist throat, his
Athenian swan-green-from-dust-to-dust-though-Romanian-
born throat.

Olga Votsi Confronts the Depths of the Sea

I hold time tightly against my flesh, like a soft-
skinned animal.
                    —Olga Votsi

Everyone sleeps the animal   at some point
          in their death-   grasp of speech.
Olga Votsi spoke of time   and the hold
it has   on the throat. Yes,   she knew the mating
habits of wolves. Of sea   creatures. Of even
the lapping of the waves. Sure,   she cried out
to Sikelianos.   To Kostis Palamas.   Even to Rilke,
Trakl, and Paul Celan.   Everyone had a clock
in their throat, she knew.   Just like the two hands
with which we are born. Turning toward   this touch
and that.

Time, an animal that quivers in the irons of your
body,   she told us. And meant   every drop
of milk   she'd collected   from the whelping dens
of wolves. How to keep   the wild woods
inside the body and still stay calm?   How to court
time yet not   sleep with the   slow
           dark   of its   death?

                    Olga Votsi knew that
Knowledge always comes as a sudden flogging on the face.
Yes, how she learned   to stare at   the empty places,
the depths.   How she interrogated   the multiple
      gaps. The blood wounds   she knew
in her knowing   knew her too well   and spat
          upon her   the sinking   of the seas.

Vassilis Tsitsanis Becomes the Legend of *Rembetika*

Stairwells and back alleys unfolded dark gaps
in his spine. Was it bouzouki music or a clock

saying, *It's dawn, Vassilis; go home*? The parlor,
full of smoke, bought women, and singing

seemed to rise from soil and mud. Even from the mud
caked upon a shoe. Look here. 1915 was only three years

before the Spanish flu and cavalry continuing on horses.
Remember that Tsitsanis was born then, as if from a termite

mound of unrest. The Greek Underground was not a sad
disposition, especially in 1935 when he came upon it and grew.

Explore your mouth, he heard as he matured.
Ask the mirror how many glances it takes to grasp

that grasping may be what's actually necessary.
Vassilis Tsitsanis ate the music of *rembetika*

as if it were a fierce flower. And Lorca
rose through the soles of Tsitsanis's own García Lorca feet

to declare moon messages as song. If you wanted
to die, this was the place. If you wanted to live, consult

the oracle of bones in your own left hand. Or a prophecy
in a row of dominoes about to collapse. A card game, perhaps,

in which one-eyed Jacks are both wild and suspicious
of the deck. Look here. Hand me a scissors-full

of ice water about to topple, a barrage of shot glasses
that seems to know us by name. After decades

performing *rembetika*, Tsitsanis opened
an *ouzeri*, which not only warmed the stomachs

of patrons with *ouzo*, but doubled as a mandolin
repair shop. *If I could have but one moment of mouth*,

he said, *I would speak as if a hookah*
of hash was bringing men together for a night

of slow talk and vision. I would speak
while boiling pans of water for the streetwalker

Photoulla, alone, frightened, about to bear another
unwanted son into Athens' dark. A stairwell,

a back alley, and a dim mouth in his spine, Vassilis
Tsitsanis beat back the broomsticks and bedstraw.

Chalice your mouth, Vassilis. Give us the sound
of wind-scrape and donkey bray as it borders the strings

of your bouzouki with long hours of the animal
night. Smoke lingers thick in the parlor

around you before trailing off into the air
coping with the agony and release of each musical note

embedded in the dead. In the almost-alive.
In the dark of the city's deafening defeat.

Vassilis Tsitsanis, After a Night of Performing
Rembetika, Sees a Photo of the Poet Anthoula
Stathopoulou and Falls Madly in Love

It was the eyes, he swore, that tore
into his chest and bore both darkness
and the other dark. Yes, he'd seen
beautiful women before but never
one who looked like a divine turtle
sunbathing a rock with shade
from the underworld. The entire Aegean
there between his heart and the places
within his ribcage he knew were swollen.
He had to sing about her, he knew.
Rembetika, the street music
of the underground—brothels, bars,
and back alley smoke. Where were her poems?
he wondered. How and why were they
lost? How might the Aegean
inside her words wash over him,
imbue? He knew only she and her poems
belonged in his mouth. Forever.
That owl-wing sweep of her midnight
hair. He put down his bouzouki.
He put down his hash pipe. He exhaled
the moon's slow smoke. Words flowed and glowed.
Slurred and blurred. Words he searched within
to uncover the meaning of all sound.
To capture the divinity
of the dead. When at only age twenty-seven
she left the body after a brief bout

of consumption. Her age—two plus seven
in numerology—adding up to nine. The sacred
number. The nine syllables within each line
of her poems. Nine beats in a *rembetika*
lament. The nine heart-wrenching lightning strikes
in his chest whenever he considered
her labored breathing. Whenever
he gazed upon her
photo and fell into the swampy dark
of her eyes. He pulled his bouzouki down
from the mantel above the burning,
easing it from the fireplace
wall, and called her
again and again back from the dead.
And every evening, hence, he sang
to her and about her and through.
In *tavernas*, in brothels,
in back alley smoke. And cafés
stirred with his words—all the housellings
of the *rembetika* mouth—the ash
of each of her lost poems he lamented
but no one seemed to know. The bouzouki dirge
of his longing. His urge that he nightly sang
again and again that she would not—
did not—die. Ever. But would remain
the everlasting life of his life.

Tasos Denegris Leaves the Crumbling of Greece
for the United States

Then they put Greece under
a microscope. Put Tasos Denegris
under a microscope. Or was it
a spectrometer?

The entomologist let loose
the Eurasian Millipede.
Then the Hissing Cockroach
from Madagascar, on which
she performed close observation
of its reproductive organs.

Then the herpetologist
set forth the Dice Snake.
Then the deadly Ohia. Then
the Balkan Whip Snake.

Tasos Denegris heard all this,
read it in the morning
maps, then planned to dissect
politics as a way to better grasp
what could be waiting in the eelgrass.
In the wind-bent of the almond
tree. The lull of the laurel. In the branch
of smoke. His poetry called forth
the undertaking of odd jobs.
Dishwasher. Street sweeper. Hodcarrier.
Clerk in the Foreign Press Division.
Even his poetry fellowship to the United States.

There was food to be had. Food to be
avoided. Tasos knew there was a night sky inside
the onion he refused to caramelize.
A darkening inside
the train whistle. A bathroom
cramped into the back of a tour bus. There,
hidden in the tenderness of his wife's
wrist, like a moonless
moon in a sun-drunk sky, he could imagine
the rest of the world. And what it might sing.

All the lab men, with their microscopes,
employed guide dogs. Adopted laboratory
mice to explore the moaning
of life in the meanderings
of the Minotaur. Revealed the Greek
crumbling of earth. The split split
splitting apart of hidden yet molecular sobbing.
And how Tasos Denegris considered
how a military regime could
somehow court autumn, blindfold
its people with leaves and brigands
of about-to-be blowing snow. Offer them
a momentary bonfire as a cigarette—
a final, comforting smoke—before leaving
the wind-swept dead of Athens, of Thessaloniki,
collapsed. Against the wall. The air
and its autumn bruise among them
refusing to move.

The Howling Lefteris Poulios Left Us With

I come to tear through silence and
to sprout in everyone.
                    —Lefteris Poulios

He saw the best minds of his generation beaten back by the
    force of wind-swept from the sea and went *taverna* to
    taverna, beret-clad, shouting poems as if the sea itself and
    all the sacred dust of despair.
Time wept until the weeping wept, and all the went and gone.
Lefteris, he knew, meant *free*, short for *Eleftherios*. Just as the
    nickname for *starlight in the mouths of the dead* might be *George*,
    or *Giorgos*, or *Here, hurt this.*

The most talented of the Generation of the Seventies, Lefteris
    Poulios lugged what he knew as his transient then-twenty-
    eight-year-old body up Mount Pendelis and—hearing a
    thunderclap of heavenly music from Apollo—selected a
    sharp rock and systematically cut off all the fingers of his
    left hand.
I must remember, he kept repeating. *Absorb. I must absorb this divine*
    visitation forever into all I have lost.

Yes, they diagnosed him as schizophrenic. Yes, the asylum
    absorbed his poems. Yes, he even threatened long-dead
    poet Kostis Palamas at the close of one poem with, *Watch*
    out for my madness, / old man: whenever it comes over me, / I'll kill
    you.
He saw the best minds of his best mind, starving, not quite
    hysterical, lost in the junta streets. The unction of each of

those bloody fingers forever emblazoned on a stone.
I wash my clothes, he wrote, *with the waters of schizophrenia.*

What do *we* wash, in the simple reading of his words? How
  might our mouths? How lush and languid our longing?
  How might the purest vowel quite our mouths? How *quit*
  and *quite* contrite in their moth-against-the-candle-flap
  quiet of a sorrowful silence?
Do we *breath*, or do we *breathe*? And how might one expand,
  bolster, or even become the rhythmic eating of the other?

Lefteris Poulios knew all this and more. The cut candles of his
  Cantos. The fact that he was born December 3, 1944—the
  day the Greek people first curved, and the Civil War
  emerged.
Sagitarrian poet. Keeper of everyone's false teeth. Cleaner of
  the bedside jar. *I am not a voice in a fenced-in world*, he had said.
  And meant it. There, in the chests of all who would listen.
  There, in the ear of his most maculate mouth. There, in the
  saliva of a sparrowhawk and bits of rainwater.

I wash my clothes. I wash You, every bit of You—he seemed to say,
  over and again through the tumbling rumble of words, the
  say-so gone wrong—*in the belligerent silence*, he told us, *that
  must cease.*

Rhea Galanaki and the Noxious Nerves of Her Throat

One morning, a starling flew into her
mouth. Moon-soaked rags seemed to ask,
Is it true the barbed-wire mouth knows
how to guard the grass on the ancient hills of Athens?
Yes, Rhea Galanaki grubbed rain from the throat
grunt of a goat. Then she spoke the stones'
slow. The stones' slow turn in the way the soil did *not*
turn. *Once, I was a horsefly*, she seemed to say,
as she stared at a stack of worthless paper
money. *Here. See my sun-bit hard. The swell*
of it and clutch. The bureaucrats and all
they kill. If the moon poured kerosene
into the mouths of the dead, the Spartans
in her spine might pass a rag-wrapped torch, scarred
with midnight char. She could dial a phone and stir the way
history asks the many hairs of the mouth
which way the ships sailed west as they bled
into the sun. Rhea's sun. As she rehearsed
the misunderstandings of words
molded into what might have been.
The Word stops here, she whispered, as if her voice
was wind whipping the willows. Once, a sparrow
settled inside her ear. Her left ear. And a bird nest
of bad weather unsettled the goats
nibbling the grass, knowing her
throat. *Here, drink here*, she told them. And coaxed water
from the gullies of each sunken star. There are wells
and ancient ways of dying, Rhea knew.
Some of which stayed with her—with us

all—as she moved through a slice
of time as if it were an apple
attached to a child's swing. An apple Rhea ate.
Daily. To calm the noxious nerves
of the throat. A throat she inherited
from the goats, the grass, from her sisters,
ancient and obscured, in the underground sulfur
caves of knowing how *not* to predict the Orphic
itch that would become her. That would become
everything her barbed voice needed. To hear.
To touch. To ache. To stay alive.

Poem in Which Natasa Hadjidhaki Becomes an Owl

Okay, it's raining again
Okay, the leaves are calling me
To the miraculous flight of her poems
Sure, there's wind in my throat
And lightning bugs in my mouth
Lightning in my ears and mouth
And moon-slips in my moist places
And, yes, wind still in my throat
When the leaves call forth the rain
And Natasa Hadjidhaki leaves her poems aside
And flies branch to branch
And absorbs the river
Absorbs the river
Into the age and ache in her throat
When it rains again
And it rains again
Because it keeps raining again and again
And the oil on her owl feathers protects her
Like the gods of Olympus throwing lightning bolts
Or icons soothing the sick
In the monasteries at Mount Athos
Oil secretions, yes, on her feathers protecting her
From the river's rising
And from all manner of darkness
Which in her owl flight she absorbs
In the way the moon absorbs her
When its milky light covers the river
The reeds
The canebrake and shadows
All that shadows the sad of her

Seven Poems of the Primordial Dark

each poem based on a painting by Giorgos Vakalo, each painting titled with a line of poetry by his wife, Eleni Vakalo

The sky that ate the sun offers it to night

We offer our lives to many things
Consider the fish bone caught in the throat
Butterflies dancing inside
The *rembetika* singer's left wrist
Once when I was a child I was the sea
Once you heard me speak you knew the depths
Of swamp light where the night heron resides
If you ask me the way south I will point north
Of your vulnerable skin
And its touch of rain and wind
The way your mouth releases moan resin
Into the soup the dandelion greens the stew
Is how the dishes become clean
How the night elongates into another night
We offer our night to the weeds the willows the canebrake
The swamp-sinking moon swallowing the dark
Once when I heard it drop through a drop
Of rain I knew how heavy the world
Once you heard me say it you knew it too

The bird that burnt and became a fish

Honestly, the plane trees frighten me with their depth

How they can drop leaves in autumn
And remain achingly alive
Suggests the contours of your body
And how starlight makes them change
Nothing endures but change, said Heraclites
And he was wise
To acknowledge wind in the throat as if it were swarms of bees
Migrating miles from Athens to Alexandria
The body of a fish becomes a bird
When the earth, when the earth turns
Through itself and becomes the soil
Of the motion of our mouths
The body of a bird can burn and become a fish
Sinking into the well-depths
Of our chest
Once it lifts itself
In its sinking
As we did many centuries before
In our brave movement from the sea

The bones of fish seem like fish

Just as the bones of the hand seem like a face
Attempting to hear itself
Heal itself in the dawn-dim dark
Of the morning mirror
I have fallen into the color green
Through the jasmine ache of its gout-like stench
Emerging as an osprey on the cliff ledge
Edging for fish
I have fallen into myself one splendid rib at a time

The way rain becomes the grass
And grass becomes sea oats and foam
The bones of fish seem to glow
When we travel the shore where they have slept
And bring their dreams into our way of staying
Still
Look at the dogs nuzzling torns of trash
To uncover the body of food belonging to a scent
The bones of the dogs seem like catgut inside
A piano
Reluctant to pluck itself to song
Just as the bones of the hand tremble and shake
When they reach into the body
Of the sea
Inside the Belovèd
In order to extract the sea

Before there were qualities there was life in the swamp

Dark places have bogs and worms and water moccasins
They seep into us just as our past leaps up unexpectedly
With fear and regret
As if all the butterflies that fascinated our child eyes
Were suddenly moths suicidal against the lamp
Cavafy sat up midnights in Alexandria contemplating his lamp
Measuring spoonfuls of kerosene
As if they were blood he might pour back into the beak
Of a dead sparrow
Embirikos too
Weighed the pebbles lodged in his heart
Against the throbbing wind

Giorgos Vakalo's swamp is much more green
Swirling
Yet partially vesicular
As if the woes of the world were pouched there
Vast but with hope
Imagine a sky rouses from the ground
Imagine a mouth about to speak
These are the things of the swamp
That ask and beg of us and blister
To come into the dark
Luminous night
Alive with the glow of bird bones and heat
With phosphorus and zinc
That give weight to the world
That rises
In hopes of drawing us down
Into sparrow flight and fane
That had been with us only briefly
But quite beautifully
Quite achingly beautiful

Butterflies make space a festival

Then there were the twelve miracles
Of spring
Each a blossoming leaf from a cypress tree
Each a step forward after the surgery
Each a word we finally found
Even if lodged in our mouths
He said I was the uncle of the moon
The wise aunt of her left wrist
The farthing and the plea

She said it was all hogwash
That my tongue needed to be clean
That my throat was a hollow bone
That birds lodged there only because it felt familiar
That even the beards of the cypress trees were suspicious
But the miracles
The twelve miracles
Each a word a phrase a way in and out of spring
The butterflies came to confirm the urge
To be fruitful and justify
The multiplying mouth
To allow the sound
To be vulnerable enough to beg, *Please*
Yesterday's today was tomorrow
Time is like that
All shift and grovel and grit
As when the caterpillar one day stops eating
Hangs upside down from a leaf or twig
And spins a silk pasture from which it will bloom
Each a step forward after the surgery of a word
Each the aunt and uncle of the moon and its plea

*Imaginary garden – Our trees after the light has
emptied them*

One plus one equals zero
If we map the galaxies with Archimedes and Pythagoras
We might appear a moment as fully human
Then we become music
A piece of perfect music empty of division and subtraction
Of sound itself
We might our mouths and ears and all manner of speak

Hidden in the hiding of it
We are left with absence we are left with trees
Just as trees are lost in us
Poplars plane trees oaks and cypresses
Which bow before us when the light gives in and grieves
Abandoning them to blurry shape and size
Here Vakalo knows the depth of the animal
Wells deep in his chest
And explores what becomes of them
After light has emptied and emerged
Poplars plane trees oaks and certain cypresses
Shift from their garden and hone
The holy work of emptying themselves
To allow the roundness of now
Allowing that roundness is their work
Now
Cartographers of the stars that they are
O Eratothenes
O Aratus
Pytheas of Massalia
Imagine a tree emptied of light
Peer into the stars and float into them
As you begin to know all you can never quite become and be

Night rises in strange shapes – None of us know them

If I asked you your name would you say *gold slipper in the mouth*?
If like the long hair of a tree I bent down into you
Would you be able to recite the close of the *Iliad* into a stone?
Able its receding rain into the bending blur of a willow?
If we arrested the word *if*
Indicted both letters for fraud

How would you respond to weather that became conditional?
To a word that could or could not be the mother of all sound?
Let's say the night rouses strange
And the shapes it exudes fascinate yet startle us
Let's say nobody understands
The fluidity of space inside
The fluidity of a word wrong-said but strong
Tell me, then
Please
If you my mouth
Tell me *into* me
Again and again the way a word the way a word might ask of it
And lightning-rinse
The most of our mouths
I ask that you ask the asking
Of it and rise with me into the thickly thin primordial dark
Comforting, quiet, confidently calm

On the Death of Miltos Sahtouris

1919–2005

So now I will never meet you, Miltos Sahtouris.
So a long time from now, July 29, 1919, will forever be
    inscribed backwards as my shame.

I will never arrive at your tiny Athens apartment, hat in
    trembling hand.
You will not open the door, squinting me my size, and tenderly
    hand me a fish covered in owl feathers, saying, *Surrealism
    freed me from many things.*

But let's say we *did* meet.
Let's say we sat smoking, and that you opened a vein and out
    came Ethiopian coffee.

Let's say the mug held blood.
That in the grounds the poems of Andreas Embirikos and
    Nikos Engonopoulos kept soaking like rags in kerosene.

And Miltiades—let me call you *Miltiades,* just once, reclaiming
    from the crows your name at birth—let's say that we went
    hand in hand to Hydra to piss on the grave of your great-
    great-grandfather, giving the old war admiral warm water
    for his bones.
Let's say the entire island turned out to see that in his chest he
    still carried a goat, that the War for Independence could
    never entirely be struck from this bone or that.

Like this sliver of eel fire the birth bag burst to become my brain.
Like the weight of Cavafy luring us all to some dark
    Alexandrian corner and trembling hand.

On my shelf, alphabetized in the manner of fire or fish, your
    books separate Ritsos from Seferis.
I see you as a kind uncle, keeping the boys from biting one
    another's wrist, instructing them on the merits of a tiny cot
    in a tiny Athens apartment where one sits day after day
    eating tiny cookies from the little neighborhood
    confectionery on the corner.

It has been written that in your *Poems, 1945–1971* you cite
    precisely 526 colors in 234 pages, that the colors of black
    (105), red (82), and white (56) predominate.
It has also been written—but never publicly revealed—that in
    my dream of meeting you, there are 453 animals silently
    roaming the room where we sit together and smoke. That
    in one hour, 43 minutes of my dreaming, the owl appears
    (for one hour, 13 minutes, 53 seconds), the donkey and
    rooster (for 16 minutes, 53 seconds; and for 12 minutes, 11
    seconds, respectively), and finally the bearded child (for a
    fleeting three seconds).

So now it is getting late, Miltos Sahtouris, and all this
    dreaming adds up to the truth that I can never dream, can
    never quite color the sky—that is—the same Chagall-horse
    blue.
You are dead or dying or about to crumble into your great-
    great-grandfather's bones or about to be reborn as some
    rare poisonous butterfly from Ethiopia or Peru or Mount
    Athos itself. And we will never meet, my friend, and a lace-
    trimmed wing will part the sea lice on my chest as I stand
    on the shore and sing, and a long time from now we will
    still never meet.

Andonis Fostieris Maps the Love of the World

If I love you it's because I love you in your pain
—Andonis Fostieris

If I love you it's because of the rain
Mayflies alive momentarily
Pouring through my body
And yours
If I love you it's because, well, *I love you*
It's because the wind the stars fragments of the blowing north
Bowing through you
Yes, *bowing* not *blowing*
As any good love must do on its humble way to loving
Even love itself
Odysseus, Achilles, Alexander, Jason
Medea, Artemis, Pandora—
All the great heroes some even gods all
Somehow flawed
Partially torn
As love is flawed and torn apart when it fails to touch
The tender places
The birds' nests in the chest
Delicately
Adding a twig or sprig of basil
How language itself stumbles in its mumbling speak
As if a mouthful of bees
As if a mouthful of bees burning off into moths
How it cannot possibly enfold the entire world
In a single vowel
Viper vesper vexed speech

In the missing the skipped
In the sentence trying to choke itself off without a period
Where even the purposeful pause of a comma
Cunningly carves itself
Out of the mouth so all words run together and merge

Just as our love for one another must mingle moments of mist
Into a new body where the moist urge we attempt falls short
And all the moorings of our journeys come loose
Wobble
And ask of and speaketh as if
Yes, I have tried so many mouths with the miracle of moons
With the swampy dark of owls sunk into the night's night
I have mastered the misery of losing the lost
The yoked-together like train cars coupling the track
The movement the howling the stitch
Midnight screech through the dark
The 2:35 a.m. to Salonika rumbling in my chest
Where striking tobacco workers lie dead since 1936
Lie dead within the sound
Of motorcycle skid and droves of the gendarmerie
Twelve dead, hundreds wounded
The 3:42 the 4:17 the 5:33
As if a line of continuous night
As if a fire scorched itself again and again
In lantern-cast through crags and curves
Of a mountain pass

O Andonis, O Andonis Fostieris
If I love you it's because I love you in your pain, you told us
Which means, of course, we must then love the entire world
The tender of it and the torn

The sudden, the sunk
As if a mouthful of moths singed off into sound
Vernal vermicular viviparous
Because the ache of the world pierces when we least respect it
A caterpillar of dirt crawling up onto us begging
We blossom into what it hopes to one day itself become
A wingèd thing living yet distinct
Into which we might flutter and fierce
Ideas lodged in the abstract in the in-between
Echoing George Seferis's cry
When he laments, *Memory hurts wherever you touch it*
Mayflies momentarily pour through our bodies
Even now when it is June
Even now in the pause the saliva grip the moist of my mouth
And yours
Odysseus, Achilles, Alexander with his flaw of wanting
The entire world at once
Medea, Artemis, Pandora
Where all the pain and murdered sons might be kept in a box
Nightjars trilling
The trials of Jason and the Argonauts
How we grumble and flesh
How language stumbles and speaks
How the stumble itself humbles us into the love loving gives
How you, Andonis Fostieris, say the way of pain
As a cobblestone path into our most belovèd
Birds' nests and how we might fly even as we settle in
In the missing the skipped
The ache of the world when we least respect
The love loving gifts us

And the touch the touch of it the clutch the extended hand

Wing-beat in the dark the slow dark slowing off
Where we humble our words
Through the mouths of moths
And repeat with Fostieris
If I love you it's because I love you in your pain
And remember if I love you it's because of the rain
Coming upon us
Slowly
Into us as it beats against the chimney the window
The cedar siding the stiff of the brain
And we come unto and speak upon and with
And chant with Seferis, *Memory hurts*
Memory hurts wherever you touch it
And sink into what's sunken and fall ourselves
Unto the world
Crying out again and again into it and through
I love you I love you I love you I love you

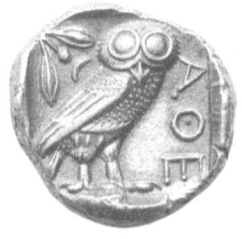

Homage to St. Dionysios

Homage to St. Dionysios

When I was a boy, you walked
Across the sea into my chest
Nono's saint
The patron saint of Zakynthos
Photos of your relics throughout our home
In the living room
The bedroom, on the chest of drawers
He brought you with him in 1916 and into my life
Forty years later
You, with your twelve miracles
Like the Hindu chakras
Six of them front and back, twelve by polarity
And the twelve lotus petals pulsing in the heart chakra
They recalled the twelve names of Surya, the sun god
And Hanuman, the monkey god, with his twelve names
You seeped into my life, St. Dionysios,
When I was six—half the number
Of each of the twelve months of the year
And every twelfth month, December 17,
We celebrated your day of rest when you left the body
Still intact in your tomb with the mixed scent
Of flowers and frankincense
Though most say your body still moves
Several nights a year across the sea with its Ionian storms
When in the morning there is seaweed inside your tomb
Your slippers thin and worn

Every night I prayed and you answered
Giving me sudden geese in the throat

The wing-beat hollow bones of their music
Disguised as the full moon bathing the twelve sections
Of our backyard boardwalk
That led to the woods' dark
And all I knew of the world
And all the world knew of me
Was a church in Greece from which you would watch over me
All those miles across, even in Indiana
Virgil's *Aeneid* in two sections came in twelve books
And the twelve principal Olympian gods of the pantheon
Preceded by twelve Titans
And later, Hercules carrying out the twelve labors

It was never a labor to love you
And I did, St. Dan, as we called you back then
My family staying Greek but learning
The English ways of the New Country
Sometimes photos of your mummified body
Heightened my six-year-old fears
But Nono told me again and again of the seaweed
And the slippers worn thin from your wanderings
And the compassion when you harbored the murderer
Of your own brother

And so, Greek Orthodoxy celebrates the twelve great feasts
And Aeschylus in *Eumenides* depicts twelve jurors
Each citizen in the play summoned by Athena
And *Christos—Christoules*—had twelve apostles
To match the twelve months of the year
The twelve signs of the Zodiac
Twelve hours in the morning, twelve after the meridian
Time merging day after day the rhythms of the human body

With starlight splitting the heavens
A body you still somehow have
Relic in the Zakynthos church that bears your name
A body that gathers seaweed when it comes ashore
The human body with twelve thoracic vertebrae
Twelve cranial nerves
The duodenum twelve inches long
The human body mirroring the music of the spheres
With its twelve pitch classes in an octave
Your twelve words liturgical in my mouth
Like the Hesychasts in the desert
Or Mount Athos
Like a Hindu chant, the name of God repeated
Mantra-like precisely twelve times

And you left the body in the twelfth month, December, 1622
And Nono left your island
For America when he was only twelve
But brought you with him in that tiny velvet bag
And *George Avgerinos*, for whom I am named,
Who first showed me your picture
Who taught me your seaweed and its stain
Contains fifteen letters
And the name *George Kalamaras* also contains fifteen letters
And my parents' divorce at age three
That brought me to live with him
Somehow brought the letters of my name back to twelve
Fifteen minus three speaking the labor
Of learning to love oneself
The work of healing into a man
Mirroring the twelve labors of Hercules
Miraculous math

Of how it all fits
How even though non-mathematical, miracles also fit
Twelve, the smallest abundant number
Twelve, the sublime number, with a perfect number
Of divisors, the sum of its divisors also perfect
And *St. Dionysios*, twelve letters
If we include the period within *St.*
Twelve, the sublime number, the *perfect* number of divisors
So that *anything* split
Can become whole
The strands of seaweed at your slippers
I imagined all those years
Tying things together from the watery depths
The twelve last seats at supper
Twelve primordial gods of Olympus
When I emerged after many lives
Freshly Greek, once again, into this body
From the body of darkness
After a long night of wandering
Through seaweed and storms

NOTES

When I have cited a text below more than once, I have provided publication information with the initial citation only.

Opening Epigraphs

George Seferis, from "In the Manner of G. S.," *Collected Poems*, expanded edition, translated, edited, and introduced by Edmund Keeley and Philip Sherrard, Princeton University Press, 1981.

George Vafopoulos, from "The End," *The Complete Poems of George Vafopoulos*, translated by Thom Nairn & Dionysia Zervanou, Dionysia Press, 1998.

Hesiod, from *Theogony, Works and Days, Shield*, translated by Apostolos N. Athanassakis, The Johns Hopkins University Press, 1983.

Epigraphs for Poems

Dimitris Antoniou, from *Six Poets of Modern Greece*, translated by Edmund Keeley and Philip Sherrard, Thames & Hudson, 1960.

Mando Aravantinou, from "Notebooks of *Script B'*" ("Excerpt A'") [*sic*]; Epameinondas Ch. Gonatas, from "Excavation"; Hector Kaknavatos, from "Saying Stones"; Yorgos V. Makris, quoted in the introduction to Chapter Thirteen; and Nanos

Valaoritis (in "Yorgos V. Makris' 'An Attempt to Become Enchanted'"), from the introduction to Chapter Thirteen: all from *Surrealism in Greece: An Anthology*, edited and translated by Nikos Stabakis, University of Texas Press, 2008.

Rita Boumi-Pappas, from "If I Go Out Walking with My Dead Friends"; Zoë Karelli, from "Persephone"; Nikos Kavvadias, from "Fog"; Melissanthi, from "The Dam of Silence"; and George Themelis, from "De Rerum Natura": all from *Modern Greek Poetry*, translated by Kimon Friar, Simon and Schuster, 1973.

Dinos Christianopoulos, from *The Body and the Wormwood* (1960–1993), translated by Nicholas Kostis (1995), quoted in "On the Origins of 'They Tried to Bury Us, They Didn't Know We Were Seeds,'" An Xiao, *Hyperallergic*, https://hyperallergic.com/449930/on-the-origins-of-they-tried-to-bury-us-they-didnt-know-we-were-seeds/. July 3, 2018.

Kiki Dimoula, from "Kiki Dimoula wows crowd at Megaron" [*sic*], Vivienne Nilan, *ekithimerini.com* (Athens Concert Hall Lecture), https://www.ekathimerini.com/culture/53015/kiki-dimoula-wows-crowd-at-megaron/. January 2007.

Andonis Fostieris, from "The Loneliness of Time," *Contemporary Greek Poetry*, translated by Kimon Friar, The Greek Ministry of Culture, 1985.

Michalis Ganas, from *Ballad*, from *A Greek Ballad: Selected Poems*, translated by David Connolly and Joshua Barley, Yale University Press, 2019.

Nikos Gatsos, from *Amorgos*, translated by Sally Purcell, Anvil Press, 1998.

Elias Petropoulos, from *Never and Nothing*, quoted in *Harsh Out of Tenderness: The Greek Poet & Urban Folklorist Elias Petropoulos*, John Taylor, Cycladic Press, 2020.

Pavlina Pampoudi, from "Alibi" (translated by Nanos Valaoritis); Nanos Valaoritis (in "Nanos Valaoritis Considers Trouble in the Tree of Life"), from "The House" (translated by Thanasis Maskaleris); and Olga Votsi, from "Time" (translated by Thanasis Maskaleris): all from *Modern Greek Poetry: An Anthology*, edited by Nanos Valaoritis and Thanasis Maskaleris, Talisman House, 2003.

Lefteris Poulios, from "I Come to Tear Through Silence," *Infinite Laughter*, translated by Kimon Friar, Realities Library (Current Greek Poets #3), 1985.

George Seferis, from "Helen," *Collected Poems*.

Angelos Sikelianos, from "When Greeks Defied the Nazis to Attend Great Poet Palamas' Funeral," Nick Kampouris, *Greek Reporter*, no translator noted, https://greekreporter.com/2022/02/28/greeks-nazis-kostis-palamas-funeral/. February 28, 2022.

Takis Sinopoulos, from "The Survivor," *Landscape of Death: The Selected Poems of Takis Sinopoulos*, translated by Kimon Friar, Ohio State University Press, 1979.

Wikipedia, quoted from and adapted for the epigraph for "Panagia."

Quotations in Poems and Other Notes
(in order of first appearance)

Section One

In "Miltos Sahtouris, Face to the Wall," the second half of the title borrows part of the title of a Sahtouris book, *With Face to the Wall*, some of which is included in Sahtouris's *Selected Poems*. In addition, *"Surrealism freed me from many things"* is a Sahtouris statement quoted in the introduction to the same volume, *Miltos Sahtouris: Selected Poems*, introduced and translated by Kimon Friar, Sachem Press, 1982.

In "'The Circle of Hours': Melissanthi's Hymnal Disposition," the first part of the title is the title of a Melissanthi poem, from *Modern Greek Poetry*. *"Behind the dam of silence, however, / the same jumble of voices"* is from her poem "The Dam of Silence," also from *Modern Greek Poetry*.

"O Pavlina!": *"I have nothing to say to no one"* is from Pavlina Pampoudi's poem "The Relationship" (translated by Nanos Valaoritis), from *Modern Greek Poetry: An Anthology*.

In "This Is Not George Seferis," the definition of "meerschaum" is adapted from the *American Heritage Dictionary*, Houghton Mifflin Company, 1979. *"All for a Helen"* is from the poem "Helen," from George Seferis, *Collected Poems*. This quote and fuller versions of this passage (see epigraph for the full quotation) also appear in the following poems: "Psychoanalytic Session in Which Andreas Embirikos Treats His Future Wife, Matsi Hatzilazarou" (Section Three), "Paul Delvaux Dreams That His Dream of Perfect Women with Classically Sculpted Beauty Is Not a Dream at All" (Section Five), and "Journey from Nemnitsa in Kyparissia" (Section Ten).

Section Three

In "Nikos Gatsos and a Certain Fatigue in the Color Green," "*Nikos was like the sweetest of grandfather elephants or the wisest and most fastidious of tortoises*" is from Peter Levi's introduction to Nikos Gatsos's *Amorgos*.

"Psychoanalytic Session in Which Andreas Embirikos Treats His Future Wife, Matsi Hatzilazarou" (Section Three) and "Solaki Census Interview with My Great-Grandmother Vasiliki Demopoulos (1862–1954)" (Section Eight): while I have experimented with writing a few "interview" poems over the years, I am grateful to John Bradley whose wonderful book *Erotica Atomica* (WordTech, 2017)—abundant with interview poems—inspired me to revisit this form for these two poems.

In "Katerina Angelaki-Rooke Contemplates the Words of Her Godfather, Nikos Kazantzakis," "*The triumph of constant loss*" is the title of her poem "The Triumph of Constant Loss," from *Contemporary Greek Poetry*.

In "George Themelis Learns to Say, *I Love You*," the first quotation, "*Outside of us things die. / Animals die from anonymity / and birds from silence*," blends two passages from Themelis's poem "Desolation." "*Whatever my soul has heard / Within me, it hears*" is from his poem "De Rerum Natura." Both poems are from *Modern Greek Poetry*. The Rilke quote, "*Only what's inside is near, the rest is far away*," is from the poem "The Island," from *The Unknown Rilke*, translated by Franz Wright, Oberlin College Press, 1983.

Section Five
In "On E. Ch. Gonatas and the Origin of the Mirrors of Our
Being," "*We shall have early fruit this year*" is from Odysseus
Elytis's poem "The Autopsy," from *Selected Poems*, translated
by Edmund Keeley, George Savidis, Philip Sherrard, John
Stathatos, and Nanos Valaoritis, The Viking Press and
Penguin Books, 1981.

In "Thusness / Dhimitris Dhoukaris Contemplates the
Grammar of the Body," the last part of the title comes from
Dhoukaris's poem "The Grammar of the Body"; "Pythia's
Words" and "The Sarcophagus" are also poem titles of his,
from *Contemporary Greek Poetry*.

In "Vowel in the Mouth: The Baptism of Eleni Vakalo," "*The Face
of Post-War Art in Greece*" is the title of one of Vakalo's books.

In "Hymns of the Body of Mando Aravantinou," "*Wherever
I travel Greece wounds me*" is from the George Seferis poem
"In the Manner of G. S.," from *Collected Poems*; "*Everything
takes place in complete silence and precision*" is from Mando
Aravantinou, from "Notebooks of *Script B '*" ("Excerpt C '") [*sic*],
some of which is included in *Surrealism in Greece: An Anthology*.

Section Seven
In "Lord Byron Discovers the Poetry of César Vallejo
Inscribed in the Delphic Stone," "*Zoë mou, sas agapo*" (or
in the Greek alphabet, "Ζώη μου, σας αγαπώ") roughly
translates to "*My life, I love you*" and approximates the
famous passage ("Zoë mou, sas agapo!")—though without
the exclamation mark—from Lord George Gordon Byron's
poem "Maid of Athens, ere we part" [*sic*], from *Selected Poems*,

Penguin Books, 1996. "*The Sacred and the Profane*" comes from the title of Mircea Eliade's book *The Sacred and the Profane: The Nature of Religion*, Harcourt Brace Jovanovich, 1959.

In "The Life of Nicolas Calas," a few "biographical" details are from the actual life of Calas, drawn from various sources.

"Soma: It is Raining, Stratis Haviaras" is dedicated to Stratis Haviaras, with gratitude for his poem "Soma"—which inspired my poem—from Haviaras's *Crossing the River Twice*, Cleveland State University Poetry Center, 1976.

In "Kostis Palamas Does Not Attend His Own Funeral," the passage—"One man shouting, *Long live the liberty of spirit!* The crowd responding, *Long live Liberty!*"—is an adaptation from a news article about Palamas's funeral, from *Greek Reporter*.

Section Eight

In "On the Deaths of My Great-Uncles Ioannis and Theodorosios Demopoulos (1918 and 1919, Respectively)," "*He saw the veins of men as a net / the gods made to catch us in like wild beasts*" is from the George Seferis poem "Euripides the Athenian," from *Collected Poems*.

In "Three Angels," the phrase "Aegean melancholy" is an adaptation of Odysseus Elytis's poem title "Aegean Melancholy," from *Selected Poems*. This poem title is also mentioned in "Journey from Nemnitsa in Kyparissia" (Section Ten). The Seferis quote, "*crucified to the wheel while she was still / beautiful,*" is from his poem "Mathios Paskalis Among the Roses," from *Collected Poems*.

Section Nine

"*On Prison and Holy Hashish*: Elias Petropoulos, the *Enfant Terrible* of Modern Greek Letters": The first part of this title comes from two separate books by Petropoulos: *On Prison* (Pleias, 1975) and *Holy Hashish* (Nefeli, 1991). However, in first reading Eve Jackson's article "Elias Petropoulos" in *The Guardian* (November 18, 2003), I conflated the two titles into one, due both to the omission of italics for book titles and to the absence of the infamous Oxford comma. I am indebted to her and to *The Guardian* for these omissions, which led me to a phantom Petropoulos title and an intriguing title for my poem!

In "D. I. Antoniou and the Nostalgia for Distant Places," "the nostalgia for distant places" is from Antoniou's poem "Tonight You Remembered," from *Six Poets of Modern Greece*.

In "Thoreau Studies Classical Greek So Long, He Wakes One Morning Only to See Homer in His Mirror," "wooded Zakynthos" alludes to Homer's description of the island as "wooded Zakynthos," from *The Odyssey*, translated by Robert Fitzgerald, Anchor Books (Doubleday & Company, Inc.), 1963. Also, several passages echo and/or deliberately misquote Thoreau from a variety of his writings.

In "Takis Sinopoulos and the Sound That Is Heard," the second half of the title and the quote in the poem, "hearing the sound that is heard," come from Sinopoulos's poem "The Survivor," from *Landscape of Death: The Selected Poems of Takis Sinopoulos*.

In "Apparently Hector Kaknavatos," the line "Apparently it could not be otherwise" comes from Kaknavatos's poem "Saying Stones," from *Surrealism in Greece: An Anthology*.

Section Eleven

In "Zephy Dharaki Becomes the Moon Becoming a Bee," "*happy blood of the moment*" is a line from her poem of the same name, "Happy Blood of the Moment," from *Contemporary Greek Poetry*.

In "Olga Votsi Confronts the Depths of the Sea," "*Time, an animal that quivers in the irons of your / body*" is from her poem "Time"; and "*Knowledge always comes as a sudden flogging on the face*" is from her poem "Knowledge." Both come from *Modern Greek Poetry: An Anthology*.

In "The Howling Lefteris Poulios Left Us With," the passages, "*Watch out for my madness, / old man: whenever it comes over me, / I'll kill you*," "*I wash my clothes with the waters of schizophrenia*," and "*I am not a voice in a fenced-in world*," come from Poulios's poems "American Bar in Athens," "The Grateful Dead," and "I Am Not a Voice in a Fenced-In World," respectively, from Poulios's *Infinite Laughter*.

In "Seven Poems of the Primordial Dark," each poem is based on a painting by Giorgos Vakalo. Each painting is accompanied by a line of poetry (which I have used as a title for each poem) by his wife, poet Eleni Vakalo, translated by Philip Ramp, from *A day with fish, animals and birds* [*sic*] ("published on the occasion of the one man show [*sic*] of G. Vakalo at the Ora Athens Cultural Center, March 1971"), Ora Athens Cultural Center, 1971. (I have rendered these titles—spacing before and after dashes, capitalization, and so forth—exactly as Eleni Vakalo has presented them.)

In "On the Death of Miltos Sahtouris," the Sahtouris quote, "*Surrealism freed me from many things*," as well as reference to the number and distribution of colors in one of Sahtouris's books, are both noted by Kimon Friar in his introduction to Sahtouris's *Selected Poems.*

In "Andonis Fostieris Maps the Love of the World," the line attributed to Seferis—"*Memory hurts wherever you touch it*"—is adapted from the passage, "I whispered: memory hurts wherever you touch it," from George Seferis's poem "Memory I," from *Collected Poems.*

Coda

"Homage to St. Dionysios": Most sources translate "Dionysios" (also "Dionysius") as "Dennis" or "Denis." However, my family from the island of St. Dionysios's birth always referred to him as "St. Dan." According to OrthodoxWiki, "Dionysius of Zakynthos" was ordained "as a priest in 1570 as *Daniel.*" In keeping with long years of family tradition, as well as with various sources confirming his ordination name, I refer to St. Dionysios in English in this poem and elsewhere as St. Dan.

The authorship of other occasional quotations in this book should hopefully be clear from the various contexts in which these quotations appear.

GLOSSARY

The following is a list of names and dates of the primary literary and artistic figures in this book. When individuals are primarily writers, I have not designated them as such. When individuals have practiced in more than one artistic discipline or profession (Giorgio de Chirico, for example), I have identified them with the artistic discipline or profession for which they are most known, unless they are equally known in more than one discipline or field. Names are listed in the order of their first appearance in poems dedicated to them or in which they figure prominently. Furthermore, several Greek writers took pen names. I have only noted a couple that might otherwise be confusing and/or are particularly relevant.

Finally, a note about Greek names: As one might expect, there are often a variety of renderings into English of both first and last names. Take George as just one example; it is an English translation of Giorgos, Giorgios, Georgios, Yorgos, Yiorgos, etc. For simplicity, I have used the version of first and last names that I have most often encountered in my reading the last forty-some years. In some cases, that might present what may seem to be an inconsistency in this book (Yorgos V. Makris, George Seferis, and Giorgos Vakalo, for example). I leave it to readers to do the deep dive on their own to discover the significance of any nuances of name variations waiting to be discovered.

Preface
Odysseus Elytis (1911–1996)

Section One
Nikos Engonopoulos (painter and poet) (1907–1985)
Jacques Prévert (1900–1977)
Nanos Valaoritis (1921–2019)
Yannis Ritsos (1909–1990)
Michalis Ganas (born 1944)
Nikos Kazantzakis (1883–1957)
Miltos Sahtouris (1919–2005)
Melissanthi (pseudonym of Eve Chougia-Skandalaki)
    (1910–1991)
Pavlina Pampoudi (born 1948)
Zoë Karelli (1901–1998)
Nikos Ghavril Pendzikis (1908–1993)
Angelos Sikelianos (1884–1951)
George Seferis (1900–1971)

Section Three
Michael Mitsakis (1868–1916)
Nikos Gatsos (1911–1992)
Matsi Hatzilazarou (1914–1987)
Andreas Embirikos (poet and psychoanalyst) (1901–1975)
Athos Dhimoulas (1921–1985)
Katerina Angelaki-Rooke (1939–2020)
Giorgio de Chirico (painter) (1888–1978)
Yorgos V. Makris (1923–1968)
George Themelis (1900–1976)
Nikos Skalkottas (classical composer) (1904–1949)
Nikos Kavvadias (poet, writer, and seafarer) (1910–1975)
Melpo Axioti (1905–1975)

Section Five
E. Ch. Gonatas (1924–2006)

Mikis Theodorakis (musical composer) (1925–2021)
Kiki Dimoula (1931–2020)
Dhimitris Dhoukaris (1925–1982)
Paul Delvaux (painter) (1897–1994)
Giorgos Vakalo (painter) (1902–1991)
Eleni Vakalo (poet, art critic, and art historian) (1921–2001)
Alexandros Panagoulis (politician and poet) (1939–1976)
Konstandinos Karyotakis (1896–1928)
Dinos Siotis (born 1944)
Yannis Kondos (1943–2015)
Mando Aravantinou (1923–1998)

Section Six
Sappho (*circa* 630 B.C.E.–*circa* 570 B.C.E.)

Section Seven
Gisèle Prassinos (1920–2015)
Lord Byron (1788–1824)
César Vallejo (1892–1938)
Constantine Cavafy (1863–1933)
Dinos Christianopoulos (pseudonym of Konstantinos
    Dimitriadis) (1931–2020)
Nicolas Calas (pseudonym of Nikos Kalamaris) (1907–1988)
Maria Efstathiadi (born 1949)
Stratis Haviaras (1935–2020)
Kostis Palamas (1859–1943)
Manolis Kalomiris (classical composer) (1883–1962)
Paul Bowles (1910–1999)

Section Nine
Elias Petropoulos (writer, folklorist, and urban historian)
    (1928–2003)

Rita Boumi-Pappas (1906–1984)

Costas Yiannoulopoulos (music journalist, radio producer of jazz and avant-garde music, and poet) (born 1948)

D. I. Antoniou (poet and sea captain) (1906–1994)

George Vafopoulos (1903–1996)

Henry David Thoreau (1817–1862)

Homer (flourished somewhere between the 12th and 8th centuries B.C.E.)

Lafcadio Hearn (Greek-Irish-Japanese writer, translator, and teacher) (1850–1904)

Thomas Merton (Trappist monk, theologian, and writer) (1915–1968)

Takis Sinopoulos (poet, painter, and physician) (1917–1981)

Jenny Mastoraki (born 1949)

Jack Spicer (1925–1965)

Dimitris Papaditsas (1922–1987)

Hector Kaknavatos (1920–2010)

Section Eleven

Zephy Dharaki (born 1939)

Olga Votsi (1922–1998)

Vassilis Tsitsanis (a founder of *rembetika*, songwriter, and bouzouki player) (1915–1984)

Anthoula Stathopoulou (1908–1935)

Tasos Denegris (1934–2009)

Lefteris Poulios (born 1944)

Rhea Galanaki (born 1947)

Natasa Hadjidhaki (1946–2017)

Andonis Fostieris (born 1953)

ACKNOWLEDGMENTS

I want to thank the editors of the following magazines and anthologies in which some of these poems first appeared, sometimes in different form:

American Literary Review: "The Sanctity"

Antigonish Review (Canada): "Dusk"

Anvil Tongue: "Alexandros Panagoulis Weighs the World One Word at a Time," "George Vafopoulos Contemplates the Sea Below His Tongue," "Maria Efstathiadi Confronts Time in the Bending of Rain," "Mikis Theodorakis Contemplates the Rise and Fall of the World," "The Song of Love," "Twelve Reasons Why Ritsos Wrote *Scripture of the Blind* Only for Those Who See," and "Vassilis Tsitsanis, After a Night of Performing *Rembetika*, Sees a Photo of the Poet Anthoula Stathopoulou and Falls Madly in Love"

The Bitter Oleander: "Closing the Parentheses"

Calibanonline: "*Christos Anesti*, Andreas Embirikos"

Contemporary Surrealist and Magical Realist Poetry (Lamar University Press): "Apparently Hector Kaknavatos," "Nikos Engonopoulos Listens to Jacques Prévert's 'Autumn Leaves' and Weeps," and "On E. Ch. Gonatas and the Origin of the Mirrors of Our Being"

Hamilton Stone Review: "Photo of My Great-Grandmother and Three Children Weeks Before They Board the Boat for the New World, *Circa* 1916" and "To Absorb the Wind"

Luna: "Lemon Seeds of Yannis Ritsos," "Looking for My Grandfather with Odysseus Elytis," and "This Is Not George Seferis"

Mondo Greco: "With Sappho at the Grave of Angeline Avgerinos"

New American Writing: "Lord Byron Discovers the Poetry of César Vallejo Inscribed in the Delphic Stone" and "Olga Votsi Confronts the Depths of the Sea"

New Orleans Review: "Miltos Sahtouris, Face to the Wall"

No Boundaries: Prose Poems by 24 American Poets (Tupelo Press): "Cavafy's Craving" (originally a prose poem)

On the Seawall: "Kostis Palamas Does Not Attend His Own Funeral"

Poetry Greece (Corfu, Greece): "Nikos Gatsos and a Certain Fatigue in the Color Green"

Pomegranate Seeds: An Anthology of Greek-American Poetry (Somerset Hall Press): "On the Death of Miltos Sahtouris"

Southwest Review: "Odysseus's Dog, Argos, Remembers What It Was Like to Be the Only One to Recognize Him Upon His Return"

Spoon River Poetry Review: "Takis Sinopoulos and the Sound That Is Heard"

Sub Rosa: "Soma: It Is Raining, Stratis Haviaras"

Sulfur Surrealist Jungle: "Seven Poems of the Primordial Dark" as well as a portfolio of poems, *"Days Come When I Forget What I'm Called": Thirteen New Poems on Greek Poets by George Kalamaras*, featuring: "George Themelis Learns to Say, *I Love You*," "Jenny Mastoraki and the Multiple Mounds of Hurt," "Katerina Angelaki-Rooke Contemplates the Words of Her Godfather, Nikos Kazantzakis," "Melpo Axioti and a Theory of Moths," "Michalis Ganas Looks at the Moon Looking at Him," "Nanos Valaoritis Considers Trouble in the Tree of Life," "Nanos Valaoritis Visits Paul Bowles in Morocco," "O Pavlina!" "Poem in Which Natasa Hadjidhaki Becomes an Owl," "A Reading from the Epistle of Gisèle Prassinos," "Rhea Galanaki and the Noxious Nerves of Her Throat," "Thoreau Studies Classical Greek So Long, He Wakes One Morning Only to See Homer in His Mirror," and "Zephy Dharaki Becomes the Moon Becoming a Bee"

Talisman: "The Bedside Table of Angelos Sikelianos," "The Death of Konstandinos Karyotakis Reborn in the Birth-Blood Poems of Dinos Siotis," "Jack Spicer Encounters Dimitris Papaditsas, Believing the Voice He Hears Late at Night Is a Radio Wave from Mars," "Kazantzakis Finds in the Mirror the Face of Zorba the Greek," "Lafcadio Hearn Dreams That He Will Be Reborn Eleven Years After His Death in the Body of Thomas Merton," "The Madness of Michael Mitsakis," "*On Prison and Holy Hashish*: Elias Petropoulos, the *Enfant Terrible* of Modern Greek Letters," "Rita Boumi-Pappas Confronts Stalin, Finally, in a Dream," "Tasos Denegris Leaves the Crumbling of Greece for the United States," "Yorgos V. Makris' 'An Attempt to Become Enchanted,'" and "Zoë Karelli Freeing the Bones of the Dead"

I also want to thank the following venues, in which some of the preceding pieces were subsequently reprinted:

Dos Madres Press: "On the Death of Miltos Sahtouris" (in the book, *Luminous in the Owl's Rib*)

The Drunken Boat: "Looking for My Grandfather with Odysseus Elytis" (as part of an online chapbook, *The Transformation of Salt*)

Leaping Mountain Press: "Soma: It Is Raining, Stratis Haviaras" (in the chapbook, *Heart Without End*)

No Boundaries: Prose Poems by 24 American Poets (Tupelo Press): "Lemon Seeds of Yannis Ritsos"

Pomegranate Seeds: An Anthology of Greek-American Poetry (Somerset Hall Press): "Looking for My Grandfather with Odysseus Elytis"

Quale Press: "Looking for My Grandfather with Odysseus Elytis," "The Sanctity," "Soma: It Is Raining, Stratis Haviaras," and "They Brought the Stone" (in the book, *Even the Java Sparrows Call Your Hair*)

Great thanks to my wife, Mary Ann Cain, for decades of love and support. I also want to thank John Bradley for being my best reader and for our sharing of Greek poetry together for decades, and I offer much gratitude to several friends for their ongoing inspiration and support, especially Eric Baus, Ray Gonzalez, Patrick Lawler, John Olson, Paul B. Roth, Lawrence R. Smith, and Lisa and John Zimmerman. I owe a huge debt of gratitude to the poet and publisher Dinos Siotis, who gifted me with many Greek journals in the early and mid-1980s—turning me onto several modern and contemporary poets at a critical juncture in my immersion in Greece's poetic tradition—and who offered important clarifications during my final phase of editing this book. I am indebted to my ancestors (those included in this book and those who are not), all of whom made it possible for me to come into the world—especially my departed parents and grandparents. I also want to thank my grandmother Helen Avgerinos and my mother, Georgina Allen, for saving and gifting me family photos throughout my life, and I extend abundant thanks to my relatives—aunt, uncle, and cousin—for filling in the gaps with essential archival family photos: Georgene Dimas, Dan Avgerinos, and Kathy Kelsey, respectively. You have all made this book alive with the eyes of family members who gave me Greece and brought it so deeply into my blood. Although I have focused this book primarily on Greek writers and my Greek family, along with other artistic and historical figures connected to Greece, I am also deeply grateful to my "other father," the late Jack Allen, an "honorary Greek" who helped raise me, providing abundant love, encouragement, and support. I also offer thanks for the love and friendship of my brothers, Perry Kalamaras and Jack Allen Jr. Finally, I want to thank Robert and Elizabeth Murphy of Dos Madres Press for taking this project on with their characteristic enthusiasm and care. Elizabeth's gorgeous renderings of icons inspired me to finish this collection, which I have worked on in one form or another for decades.

About the Author

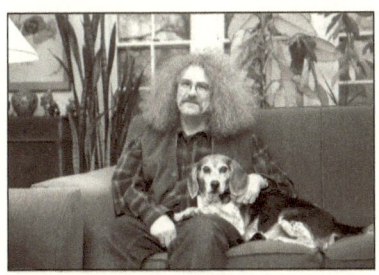

GEORGE KALAMARAS is former Poet Laureate of Indiana (2014–2016). He is the author of twenty-one collections of poetry—thirteen full-length books and eight chapbooks—as well as a critical study on language theory. A recipient of various national and state prizes for his poetry, he spent several months in India in 1994 on an Indo-U.S. Advanced Research Fellowship. In addition to his publications in the United States, his poems have appeared in print journals in Africa, Asia, Europe, and Latin America and have been translated into Bengali and Spanish. He is Professor Emeritus of English at Purdue University Fort Wayne, where he taught for thirty-two years. George and his wife, writer Mary Ann Cain, have nurtured beagles in their home for nearly thirty years, first Barney, then Bootsie, and now Blaisie. George, Mary Ann, and Blaisie divide their time between Fort Wayne, Indiana, and Livermore, Colorado, in the mountains north of Fort Collins.

www.ingramcontent.com/pod-product-compliance
Lightning Source LLC
Chambersburg PA
CBHW021611120626
46545CB00001B/168